Team-Managed Facilitation:

*Critical Skills for Developing
Self-Sufficient Teams*

Dennis C. Kinlaw, Ed.D.

Amsterdam • Johannesburg • London
San Diego • Sydney • Toronto

Library of Congress Cataloging-in-Publication Data

Kinlaw, Dennis C.
   Team-managed facilitation: critical skills for developing self-sufficient teams / Dennis C. Kinlaw
   p.cm.
   Includes bibliographical references and index.
   ISBN 0-88390-338-5
   1. Work groups.   I. Title
   HD66.K563   1992   92-22811
   658.4'02   CIP

Pfeiffer & Company • 8517 Production Avenue • San Diego, CA 92121-2280
            (619) 578-5900   FAX (619) 578-2042

Dedication

*For Stella with love and thanks
for making this book and my life easier.*

Preface

This is my third book about teams. In the first book, *Developing Superior Work Teams*, I describe a model for superior teams that grew out of a five-year study of teams and their performance. The second book, *Continuous Improvement and Measurement for Total Quality*, provides a rationale for team-centered continuous improvement and describes a comprehensive model and process for designing improvement-and-measurement projects. These previous books deal with the total development and work of teams. In this third book about teams, I am concerned with a single (but critical) aspect of the life and work of teams: their meetings.

It is apparent that teams must meet and that the total performance of teams is influenced by the quality and success of their team meetings. This book explains how team meetings can be greatly improved by means of the process of team-managed facilitation.

This book carries forward the underlying assumptions of my earlier books. These assumptions are that teams:

1. Are the primary units of performance and the great untapped source for new ideas, innovation, and continuous improvement in organizations;

2. Are capable of managing every aspect of their own development and performance; and

3. Require clear, cognitive models for developing themselves and managing their performance.

The advent of team formation and team development as major strategies for organizational development and continuous improvement has created a need for the competent facilitation of team meetings that is far greater than at any time in the past. This need is, however, not just large; it is different.

Organizations need teams that are more and more self-sufficient in managing their own development. For teams to be self-sufficient, they must have many new skills. One such set of skills is the ability to facilitate their own meetings.

Organizations need the skills for team formation and development to be fully developed and generously distributed among all their people. They need to move away from the expensive habit of making facilitation a special skill and developing facilitation as a special job. They need to move toward the cost-effective practice of making facilitation a general job skill that all team members have. This book presents a new understanding of facilitation to meet these new needs. In writing this book, I have returned to the root meaning of "facilitate": to *make easy or easier.*

Everything in this book has been tested many times over in helping teams to conduct successful meetings and in teaching people how to facilitate successful team meetings.

The bias that I exhibit throughout this book is that the facilitation of meetings can be judged only by its results, i.e., did it make the work of the team easier and more successful? This represents something of a break from traditional theories and understandings of what facilitators and facilitation are. I do not accept, for example, the traditional notion that facilitators must remain distant from the team's work and uninvolved in its conversations. Also, I do not accept the typical belief that facilitators are only concerned with "process."

I develop my understanding of facilitation by starting with the question of what makes a successful team meeting. I then define facilitation as doing what has the highest probability of making it easy or easier for the team to be successful.

The development of this book was greatly facilitated by the thoughtful help that I received from my wife, Stella, and from my Canadian colleague, Bob Fenske. I thank them for the time that they spent in reviewing my manuscript and for the many useful recommendations that they made to improve it. I am also grateful to the hundreds of teams and facilitators with whom I have worked over the past twenty-five years and who have all contributed to my formulation and clarification of the idea of team-managed facilitation.

Finally, I want to acknowledge the work of Arlette C. Ballew, my editor at Pfeiffer & Company. This is the fourth book of mine that Ms. Ballew has edited, and she has made a major contribution to the final value of each.

Table of Contents

Introduction

This book presents a model for facilitating team meetings that differs substantially from those that traditionally have been offered. It focuses on performance and the bottom line. It is particularly well-fitted for use in organizations that are committed to using teams as the foundations of their total quality and continuous improvement initiatives. It has special relevance and utility for self-managed teams.

I believe that the traditional view of team facilitation no longer is very useful and leads to the following kinds of problems:

1. It makes the job of the facilitator unnecessarily complex and tends to "professionalize" the role;

2. It tends to focus the facilitator on interpersonal relationships and group communications rather than on output and performance;

3. It fails to provide meeting facilitators with clear, rational models that they can use to structure their actions and interventions; and, ultimately,

4. It wastes the resources of organizations on poorly designed and ineffective training programs that fail to equip people with the understanding and skills that are needed to help teams to reach high levels of proficiency in their various types of meetings.

I have written this book to provide a new understanding of team facilitation that is particularly relevant to the general movement of organizations toward team-managed operations and cultures. This book proposes that the facilitation of meetings, just like every other task, role, or job, should be viewed as an element in team performance whose over-arching function is to contribute to team formation, team development, and the self-sufficiency of the team.

THE NEED FOR A NEW APPROACH TO FACILITATION

Organizations need an understanding of team facilitation that:

- Reflects a commitment to minimizing overhead and running lean;
- Can support the immense effort of team formation and development that is now characteristic of most organizations;
- Clearly is congruent with forming teams that are responsible for their own performance; and
- Leads to training that, in turn, leads to better team meetings and improvement in overall team performance.

Organizations need facilitation training that creates the following conditions:

- Provides people with a cognitive understanding of facilitation that they can apply with a minimum amount of practice;
- Gives people tools that are true functional resources that can be referred to and used as needed; and

- Is appropriate for people who function as facilitators, regardless of how experienced they are or how much time they spend as facilitators.

The purpose of this book is to provide a model for and understanding of the skills of team facilitation that meet all of the above conditions.

THE RESOURCE OF FACILITATION

Teams and teamwork generally are viewed as key strategies for achieving total quality performance. Team formation is taking place from top to bottom and across every interface in most organizations as these organizations respond to the relentless demand to build customer satisfaction, improve work processes, and upgrade the performance of their suppliers (Kinlaw, 1991; 1992).

The formation of teams and their ongoing development require a variety of supports and resources, e.g., good management-team models, team-managed personnel practices, communication-skills training, problem-solving-skills training, etc. In addition to these resources, however, there is one more that can play a critical role in the formation, development, and performance of teams. This resource is skilled facilitation.

FACILITATION: PROFESSION, JOB, AND ROLE

The resource is *skilled facilitation* and not *skilled facilitators*. The function of facilitating team meetings can exist as a profession, job, or role (Figure Int-1). Facilitation differs as a profession, job, or role, primarily in the amount of time

Level	TIME	NEEDS	COMPETENCIES
Profession	Varies by degree of emphasis that facilitation has in consultant's practice	• Therapy • Personal Growth • Team Building • Team Development	Broad competencies based on extensive academic education
Job	Varies as job of facilitation is part-time or full-time	• Team Building (perhaps) • Team Development	Technical competencies based on considerable special training and extensive practical experience
Role	Varies with emphasis team places on using designated facilitator	• Team Development	Technical competencies based on practical training and practice

Figure Int-1: Facilitation As Profession, Job, and Role

spent, the kinds of needs addressed, and the kinds of competencies required.

Time spent can vary from moments (as when a team member makes an input that facilitates the team's movement toward a goal) to days (as when a professional works with a team over an extended period of time in an intense team-building session).

The kinds of needs that facilitation addresses will vary from helping teams with simple problem solving (e.g., following some logical procedure or designing a project to improve performance) all the way to helping people to resolve complex human issues (e.g., overcoming serious interpersonal conflict or gaining insight for personal growth). As far as the typical task team is concerned, these needs can be viewed as varying from team development to team building. Figure Int-2 describes the difference between team development and team building. I have developed the distinctions between these two in some detail in *Developing Superior Work Teams: Building Quality and the Competitive Edge* (Kinlaw, 1991).

The competencies required for facilitation naturally vary with the needs addressed. Needs for therapy and personal growth can be properly addressed only by professionals who can draw on a large body of theoretical knowledge obtained from extensive academic preparation.

I consider facilitation a *role* when a person acts as a facilitator for brief or designated periods of time. Any time that a team member makes a facilitative input during a meeting, that member is in the role of facilitator. Also, a person may be placed in the role for a specified period of time—as when a team appoints one of its own members as a designated facilitator. After the period is over, the role may be taken over by a different person, or the need for a designated facilitator may no longer exist. Facilitation as a role can be observed in teams in which the role is rotated from meeting to meeting or in which a designated facilitator is used for a particular activity or exercise. Facilitation as a role also can be observed in training sessions during

TEAM BUILDING	TEAM DEVELOPMENT
Deficit focuses on blocks to team's performance	Focuses on positive opportunities for continuous improvement
Short-term concern to fix immediate, severe, interpersonal problems	Long-term concern to set up resources, structures, and processes for long haul
Intense, usually varies from several hours to several days	Diffused and ongoing, part of the team's routine
Typically targets problems in relationships	Typically targets problems in resources, structures, and processes
Typically requires the help of a professional facilitator (or at least a highly experienced one)	An ongoing process that every team member can be trained to manage

Figure Int-2: Team Building and Team Development

which one person in a learning group acts as facilitator during an activity or for a series of activities.

Another example of facilitation as a role occurs in organizations when people have become known for their skill as facilitators even though facilitation is not part of their official job descriptions. They have no formal recognition as facilitators in the organization's structure. These people are known by others to be available and to serve as facilitators when requested and as the responsibilities of their regular jobs permit.

Facilitation sometimes exists as an official full-time job or as one responsibility among others in a single job. During the rise and fall of quality circles, a number of organizations added full-time facilitators to their staffs. The same process has begun to occur again with the advent of total quality management (TQM). It has become more and more typical, however, that people with already existing full-time jobs are being trained as part-time facilitators. Training a cadre of part-time facilitators is a typical strategy among the training and consulting houses who are assisting organizations through the full sequence of planning and initiating programs in TQM.

In applying the term *profession* to facilitation, I refer to those consultants, trainers, and therapists who function as facilitators on a regular basis and who present themselves as having special expertise as facilitators. These professional facilitators may be involved in activities ranging from strategic planning, through team building, to personal growth or therapy. Figure Int-1 provides an outline of the differences that exist in facilitation as a profession, job, and role.

Because this book is about facilitation, anyone who serves as a facilitator will find information and ideas here that can be applied to the profession, job, or role of facilitator. The book is, however, focused on task teams and on facilitation as a team-managed activity.

TEAM-MANAGED FACILITATION

The view of facilitation presented in the pages that follow is that facilitation is empirical, structured, explicit, and thoroughly rational. *Most of all, facilitation is a team responsibility and should be viewed as a team-managed activity.*

Empirical

The approach to facilitating team meetings that is presented in this book is derived from a Model for Successful Team Meetings that has been tested with hundreds of teams over a period of ten years. I have used the model as my primary tool for facilitating the meetings of senior executives involved in strategic planning. I have used it to form teams, to develop teams, and to help teams that were involved in designing various improvement projects. I have used it consistently to support team learning in the many different kinds of training programs that I have conducted over the years.

The model is, first of all, based on my own observations and experiments as a facilitator. The model has, in addition, been thoroughly tested as a tool for training teams to manage their own facilitation. In later pages, I will show how the model can be used to train all team members to be successful facilitators.

Structured

A second characteristic of facilitation that is proposed in this book is that it is structured. This does not mean that it is rigid. It means that it has a definable shape or form that can be clearly described and used.

Facilitation is structured, first, because it depends on the Model for Successful Team Meetings (Figure 2-2). The goal of facilitation is to bring the model to life and to help a team understand and use the model for its own benefit. Facilitation also is structured in the sense that it uses a variety of rational problem-solving sequences and tools in helping teams to perform their tasks and to achieve their goals.

Explicit

Facilitation should be self-evident and transparent. My view is that every member at a team meeting should be aware of how well the meeting is being facilitated. If a designated facilitator is used, the team should know what the designated facilitator is doing at all times.

The reasons for every intervention made by a team member or designated facilitator should be apparent to every team member. In addition, team members and designated facilitators should keep their teams *conscious* of what their teams are doing and of what they are not doing. They should help their teams to get on with doing what they need to do.

For example, member facilitators should perform tasks such as keeping the team aware of the goals it intends to reach and aware of the rational processes and models that it is trying to use. As a team progresses through its work during a meeting, member facilitators should keep the team aware of just how well it is achieving its goals and how well it is using its processes and models.

Keeping the team conscious of what it is doing and keeping it aware of what the facilitator is doing are absolute requirements if the team is to take responsibility for its own facilitation, i.e., make facilitation a team-managed process.

I remember being in a group some years ago in which the facilitator's major intervention was to produce one model or another to help us to understand what we *already* had done. He unveiled the Johari Window to show us how we had been giving and requesting feedback. We were presented with Leland Bradford's (1978) cyclical model of "Group Formation and Development" to show us that our phase of "confronting a difficult problem" was inevitable and that all was going according to plan. Sooner or later we were exposed to most of the popular models of the day— *but all after the fact.*

The unexpressed bias that often is built into facilitation is that the facilitator is doing something that is so profound, so mysterious, or so esoteric, that only the facilitator can fully understand what is going on. This bias places control with the facilitator as the expert or guru. *The description of facilitation that will be presented in this book is that facilitation is a team responsibility and should be managed by the team.* Such management may occur through the competent interventions of any team member or of the team's designated facilitator.

Rational

When I describe facilitation as rational, I mean the following:

- It has a high level of objectivity. It can be described and understood. It can be invoked deliberately and used to help structure a conscious decision.
- Its usefulness can be measured by rigorous criteria. Because it can be measured, it can be improved.

- It consists of models, tools, and skills that can be taught and learned.

When we view facilitation as a primarily rational process, we will rely as much on team members' capacities to learn from cognitive models as we will rely on their capacities to learn from their experience. The rational view of facilitation leads team members and designated facilitators to describe *what is likely to happen*, not only *what has happened.* It will lead them to develop clear road maps with their teams and will provide them with the tools to regulate their progress and to follow these maps.

If we think of facilitation as a rational process, we will focus on the fundamental job of facilitation, i.e., *to make things easy.* Facilitation is what the team does to help itself succeed at its tasks and goals. When we translate this notion of making things easy into specific functions, we can define the job of member facilitators during a meeting to be that of helping a team to:

- Identify and anticipate blocks to its performance;
- Overcome blocks to its performance; and
- Search for and find better ways to perform all of its tasks.

The rational view of facilitation proposes that there is no value inherent in pain. This view does not accept the idea that a team is able to develop only by traversing a predestined and tortuous route filled with mistakes, failures, and confusion.

My view of facilitation accepts as a given that we know what is required for highly efficient and effective meetings and that we have a variety of models and tools that can be understood and used. The rational view proposes that team members and their designated facilitators should use these models and these tools with deliberation and by conscious decision.

Team-Managed Facilitation

All of the foregoing characteristics that I associate with facilitation, i.e., empirical, structured, explicit, and rational, are preconditions if, as I propose, facilitation is to be team-managed. Team-managed facilitation suggests that team members (individually and collectively) should view themselves as:

- Responsible for the team's development and performance and the aggregate of understandings, decisions, and tasks that make up that development and performance; and
- Responsible for the success of every team meeting.

In team-managed facilitation, facilitation is always a role. It can never be completely someone else's job. It is the team's job.

The role of facilitation sometimes will be rotated and shared among a variety of people. These people may be permanent team members or they may come from other parts of the organization or even from outside the organization. But even though the role may move around, the responsibility never does. The responsibility is always the team's.

Team-managed facilitation means that the team always is directly involved in facilitating its own meetings. Individual members, skilled in a common discipline of facilitation, will initiate a variety of interventions to help the team toward its goals. For such interventions to take place, the entire team must be operating from a common under-standing of facilitation and effective team meetings. For facilitation to be team-managed, the team first must have a common view of facilitation that is empirical, structured, explicit, and rational.

When team-managed facilitation is fully functioning in a team, the requirement for individuals to occupy the role of facilitator becomes less and less frequent. An individual who is serving in the role of facilitator should be viewed as functioning in a temporary role required by some special circumstance. Team facilitation, in fully developed teams, most often can be managed through the spontaneous and informal interventions of all team members.

It should be apparent from the foregoing paragraph that team-managed facilitation is a view of facilitation that is fully congruent with the popular notion of empower-ment. It is particularly appropriate at a time in which inde-pendent and self-managed teams are becoming more and more common in organizations.

THE FUNCTIONS OF TEAM-MANAGED FACILITATION

The functions of team-managed facilitation are derived from the Model for Successful Team Meetings (Figure 2-2). These functions help the team to:

- Develop its maximum potential by identifying and gathering the required resources;
- Develop its maximum potential by building the struc-tures it requires to function efficiently and effectively;

- Incorporate into its meetings rational processes that support task achievement;
- Communicate during team meetings so that resources, structures, and processes are used to their full potential; and
- Develop clarity about its tasks as well as sufficient information to solve problems and make decisions.

These functions and the skills required to perform them are described in subsequent chapters.

TRAINING

In developing and supplying the resource of facilitation to its teams, an organization must make several key decisions. It must, for instance, decide whether facilitation will be a profession, job, or role.

Suppose that it decides that facilitation is a job; it then must decide how extensive the job of facilitator will be. Will it be a full-time or a part-time job? Will it be a temporary or permanent assignment?

Assuming that an organization has made a commitment to team formation and development and intends to support this commitment with capable facilitators, the decision that can most directly affect the success of its teams is: how will facilitators be trained? This may be the most important decision that an organization will make about facilitation.

The way in which facilitators are trained will determine not only *how well they do their jobs* but, more importantly, it will determine *what job they will do.*

People who are trained in traditional approaches to facilitation will not facilitate in the same way as a person who is trained in the team-managed approach. Only those persons who are trained in the latter will persistently and consciously view facilitation as a fully collaborative activity of themselves and the team. Only those persons who take a team-managed approach to facilitation will ensure that the team remains fully conscious and knowledgeable at all times of what it is doing and what it is about to do. Only those persons who are trained in team-managed facilitation will consciously help the team to transfer responsibility for facilitation from themselves to the team. Only team-managed facilitation can finally lead to fully self-reliant, self-regulating, and self-managed teams.

PURPOSES OF THIS BOOK

This book is intended to do the following:

- To describe a team-managed approach for facilitating team meetings that is fitted to the current organizational realities of intense and pervasive team development;
- To describe a Model for Successful Team Meetings that forms the foundation for facilitating and training for facilitation; and
- To describe the skills that team members need to function as facilitators.

WHO CAN USE THIS BOOK

This book has been written with an intent to serve the needs of several kinds of readers.

The first group of people who will find this book to be useful are team members who want to become more self-sufficient and decision makers who want self-sufficient teams in their organizations.

The next group of people who will find this book useful are team members who want to improve their competencies for facilitating their own team meetings. This book does not assume that the reader has any prior knowledge of team facilitation or the dynamics of team meetings.

A third group of people who will find help in this book are those who are responsible for designing or delivering training for teams and team facilitators. The book can become a major resource for such training. I have included the outline of a design for team-managed facilitation in the Appendix.

A final group of people who will find this book of use are experienced facilitators and professionals from every field who function as facilitators. This book offers a highly cognitive and structured approach to team facilitation. This approach includes many ideas for carrying out the various functions of facilitation that the most experienced facilitators might well consider as alternatives or additions to their current practices.

DEFINITIONS

A number of terms are used with great frequency throughout this book. It is important to specify the exact meaning that I intend each of these terms to carry.

- **Facilitation.** Interventions made by any person during a team meeting that help the team to meet certain criteria for success. Facilitation can exist only as helpful interventions. Without help there is no facilitation.

- **Facilitator.** Any person who makes helpful interventions during a team meeting. This person may be identified as the team's facilitator or may be a team member.
- **Designated Facilitator.** Any person whom the team selects to occupy the role of facilitator for a specific period of time. A temporary responsibility that may be filled by a team member or by a person from outside the team.
- **Intervention.** Any statement or action made by a facilitator during a team meeting. Interventions may take the form of suggestions, observations, the use of structured problem-solving tools, feedback, etc.
- **Team.** Any group of people who meet to perform some task and whose group: (1) could become a team if its members chose to do so; (2) is small enough so that members can interact fully with one another; and (3) could make decisions by consensus—if it chose to do so.

ORGANIZATION OF THE BOOK AND SUMMARIES OF CHAPTERS

The general design of this book is to describe the relationship of team meetings to team development and performance, to describe the special characteristics of team-managed facilitation, to develop a Model for Successful Team Meetings, and then to show how the model can be used as the foundation and framework for facilitating teams. After I have given an overview of team-managed facilitation in the first two chapters, I provide a demonstration of what team-managed facilitation actually looks like in Chapter 3.

The demonstration takes the form of a behavioral dramatization.

A behavioral dramatization is, like any play, larger than life. The dramatization is a true replication of what actually occurs in teams that use team-managed facilitation, but it is more. It is a condensation of hundreds of team meetings and hundreds of experiences with team-managed facilitation. This dramatization provides a reference and resource for the rest of the book. In following chapters, as I discuss a specific aspect of team-managed facilitation, I will refer to the dramatization to illustrate what I am discussing.

A NOTE ABOUT TOOLS

There are a great many structured problem-solving tools that are useful in facilitating team meetings. Among such tools are:

- Brainstorming;
- Nominal group technique;
- Cause-and-effect diagrams;
- Charting work processes; and
- Structured feedback.

I have not included a description of problem-solving tools in this book because such descriptions are readily available in a variety of already published sources. I have, for instance, described many structured problem-solving tools in my book *Continuous Improvement and Measurement for Total Quality: A Team-Based Approach* (Kinlaw, 1992) and have shown how these tools can be used in the process of designing and implementing improvement projects. The reader who is unfamiliar with these tools is encouraged to consult any of the published sources for such tools in the "References and Resources" at the end of this book.

A summary of the content of each chapter is provided below.

Chapter 1. Teams, Their Meetings, and Facilitation

This chapter defines teams and discusses the role that team meetings have in team formation, team development, and team performance. It also outlines the functions of facilitation in team meetings and team development.

Chapter 2. The Foundation: A Model for Successful Team Meetings

Teams are much more than their meetings, but meetings have a central function in total team performance. This chapter develops a Model for Successful Team Meetings and shows how it can be used as the framework for facilitation and as a guide for ensuring highly productive team meetings.

Chapter 3. Team-Managed Facilitation in Practice: A Behavioral Dramatization

This chapter provides a demonstration of what the other chapters in the book describe. It contains a behavioral dramatization of team-managed facilitation. The dramatization illustrates the key behaviors that are required of facilitators to create the meetings that conform to the design given in the Model for Successful Team Meetings.

Chapter 4. Core Competencies for Team-Managed Facilitation

Team-member facilitators (whether designated or not) must be able to use the Model for Successful Team Meetings and must have several sets of other core skills. This chapter identifies these skills and describes their use.

Chapter 5. Facilitation and the Roles of Leaders and Managers

This chapter provides a convenient summary of key points covered in the book and connects facilitation to the emerging roles of and requirements for today's leaders and managers.

Appendix. Outline for Team-Managed-Facilitation Training

I have included in the Appendix the outline of a two-day training program in team-managed facilitation. This outline makes extensive use of the Model for Successful Team Meetings and describes a variety of exercises for developing facilitation skills.

Chapter 1

Teams, Their Meetings, and Facilitation

In this chapter, I will provide the basis for understanding what team-managed facilitation is and how it differs from the ways in which facilitation has been understood and used in the past. The specific topics that I will discuss are:

- The meaning of team;
- The general characteristics that determine the many different kinds of teams that meet;
- The different kinds of tasks that teams may perform when they meet;
- The role that team meetings play in team development and performance;
- What determines the need to use a designated facilitator;
- The goals of facilitation; and
- The meaning and function of the interventions of facilitation.

THE MEANING OF TEAM

I use the word "team" to refer to any small group that meets periodically to undertake various tasks. I am not restricting the definition to a group that has developed into a highly collaborative and integrated set of members. I use "team" to describe any group of people who meet the following criteria:

1. The group could become a team or even a superior team, if it chose to do so (Kinlaw, 1991);

2. The group meets at times to perform some type of task;

3. The group is small enough so that its members can interact fully with one another to make decisions and solve problems; and

4. The group is small enough to make decisions by consensus—if it chose to do so.

KINDS OF TEAMS

Teams can vary in at least the following ways (Kinlaw, 1992):

- They may be "natural" work teams within the normal organizational structure or they may be formed for a special reason;

- Membership may be voluntary or involuntary;

- The team's tasks may be assigned, or the team may have the freedom to select or order its own tasks;

- Teams may cross internal organizational boundaries and include people from different organizational units or teams may exist within a single work unit;

- Teams may cross external organizational boundaries and include people from different organizations or teams may exist within the same company; and

- Teams may be self-managed or have an assigned leader.

Teams, of whatever kind, present opportunities for improvement. Teams meet. Each team meeting is a potential opportunity for improvement. Each team meeting is, therefore, a potential opportunity for facilitation.

KINDS OF TASKS

We are concerned primarily with the facilitation of the meetings of task teams. Our focus is on those tasks that teams can perform at their meetings. We are not concerned with the whole world of team development and performance; i.e., the multitude of tasks that team members perform as part of their work day and their life together when they are not meeting as a team. A partial list of the tasks that teams can perform at their meetings is:

- **Develop the team**, e.g., develop benchmarks regarding the team's performance, evaluate team meetings, set norms for team meetings, design team-improvement projects.
- **Make decisions**, e.g., about the budget, hiring, awards, selecting contractors, setting goals, agreeing on schedules, identifying improvement opportunities, setting priorities.
- **Solve problems**, e.g., analyze data and identify causes, modify work processes, reallocate resources to respond to changes and crises, design alternatives and contingencies.
- **Share information**, e.g., about anticipated problems, status of current activities, projected changes in policies, team successes and achievements, training opportunities.

- **Learn**, e.g., through discussion of a new procedure, briefings about new technologies, presentations from experts and specialists.
- **Design improvement projects**, e.g., to measure quality of services and products, to improve customer satisfaction, to improve work processes.

During the dynamic interaction and movement that takes place during any team meeting, tasks rarely exist in clean, separate categories. Also, there are many subtasks that must be achieved in order to complete a central task. To complete a strategic plan, a team might need to complete the subtasks of refining a mission statement, developing a new vision statement, revising scans of its internal and external environments, and so on. To revise its environmental scans, a team might complete a number of information-developing tasks by using brainstorming or another idea-generating tool—another subtask.

One key function of facilitation is to help the team to identify concretely what tasks it intends to complete and the various subtasks that are associated with that task. To do this, a team must stay conscious of what subtask it is performing at any moment and how this subtask is related to the larger task. A principle contribution that facilitation makes to a team's success is *to keep the team conscious at all times of what it is doing.*

THE ROLE OF MEETINGS IN TEAM DEVELOPMENT AND PERFORMANCE

Meetings are one of the many activities that teams employ to strengthen themselves as teams and to get their jobs done.

Meetings may be a primary activity of teams (as in the case of teams that are formed to investigate an accident, select a contractor, develop a policy, or make promotion selections). Meetings are a primary activity of most committees and councils.

Meetings also may be an ancillary activity of teams, e.g., weekly staff meetings, crew meetings, meetings to communicate the status of a project, strategic-planning meetings, and budget-planning meetings.

Within the framework of total quality management programs, team meetings are the venue for the special functions of designing, implementing, and managing improvement projects (Kinlaw, 1992). For self-managed teams, meetings become an indispensable tool for carrying out most of the team's management responsibilities (Orsburn, et al., 1990).

From the foregoing description, it becomes apparent that:

- The role that team meetings play in the team's performance varies greatly; and
- Some teams exist only because they meet, and other teams would exist whether they met or not.

Three useful generalizations that we can make about team meetings are that they always:

- Present an opportunity to perform a task;
- Present an opportunity for the team to develop itself as a team; and
- Present an opportunity for improving present and future team meetings.

FACILITATION: NEEDS AND OPPORTUNITIES

Attempts at facilitation are present to some degree at every team meeting. Someone always will try to further the progress of a team toward a goal. These attempts at facilitation often are intuitive, random, and undisciplined. Intuitive and random facilitation is very inefficient and wasteful of time and resources.

All teams can benefit from disciplined facilitation. The need for a designated facilitator does not depend on the kind of team involved. The need for a designated facilitator depends on: (1) the level of development of the team and its capacity to manage its own facilitation; (2) the level of difficulty in the tasks that the team is undertaking; and (3) the competencies that the team has for facilitating its own meetings.

Level of Development

Teams that are quite underdeveloped always can benefit from the services of a designated facilitator. This is why teams at early stages of formation receive such benefit from designated facilitators. Early stages of team development, it should be noted, do not correspond directly with the time that a group has been in existence.

Over the past five years, I have led a total quality management seminar for NASA's Kennedy Space Center. Some five thousand people have attended the seminar to date. People from NASA's civil service and NASA's contractors attend the seminar in teams. These teams are of the following kinds:

Intact Work Teams. People who work together daily and who, most often, have a supervisor or lead.

Management Teams. A manager and his or her staff and direct reportees, including secretaries, deputies, technical assistants, etc.

Interface Teams. Groups that must work together across some organizational boundary to get the job done. Interface teams can exist within the same organization, e.g., between design engineering and manufacturing, and between different organizations. They include *customer-supplier teams* and *supplier-customer teams.*

Project Teams. People put together to complete a specific task within a designated period of time. Examples are design teams, procurement teams, flight-project teams, and construction teams.

Special-Improvement Teams. Can have all sorts of titles and descriptions, including quality-action teams, process-improvement teams, cross-functional teams, quality-management teams, etc.

Network Teams. People who work together, share information, and participate in related tasks, but rarely see one another. Most of their business is transacted by telephone, electronic mail, or paper. A good example is the network of secretaries that links together all sorts of processes and actions in organizations.

Committees and Councils. Permanent and temporary groups such as EEO councils, source evaluation boards, awards committees, child-care committees, promotion boards, etc.

The total quality management seminar has special objectives related to continuous improvement, assessment, and measurement. To achieve these objectives during the two days of the seminar, each team that attends the seminar (from the ten or so different companies involved) has a designated facilitator. These designated facilitators attend a special training program prior to their participation in the seminar.

Designated facilitators are used in this seminar because we do not know in advance what levels of development and performance have been reached by the teams that will be attending. It is apparent that the teams that come to the seminar are in various stages of development that have little to do with how long they have existed. At one extreme, we may have intact work groups that have been in existence for many years, but which have never made the conscious decision to become teams. Such groups often have no common goals, no clear set of core values, and no extensive experience of collaborative behavior. When these teams attend the seminar, they are at the threshold for beginning their development.

Other teams that attend the seminar may have been formed for a special improvement initiative and have been in existence for only a few weeks or months. These teams, however, often already function at a very high level of development.

The need for facilitation is, first of all, a function of the level of team development. The level of development can be assessed in a number of ways. One strategy is to use a model or set of variables that reflects what the best teams are like and to develop benchmarks of team development (Kinlaw, 1991).

Difficulty of the Task

The need for a designated facilitator depends first on the level of development of the team. The need for a designated facilitator also depends on the difficulty of the task that the team is trying to perform.

The difficulty of a task is relative to the competence of the team to perform it. An executive group that is meeting for the first time to do strategic planning usually can benefit from the services of a designated facilitator. A team that is putting together for the first time an organization's total quality goals and plan usually needs a facilitator. Teams that are learning a new quality-management technique such as quality deployment, control charting, assessment of customer satisfaction, or work-process simplification are well-advised to use a designated facilitator.

One of the mistakes that teams often make is that they presume that they have certain competencies and do not require the services of a designated facilitator. I know of one senior manager who has "outlawed" the use of facilitators along with team training of any kind. His bias is that "my people know how to function as a team. All I have to do is give them an assignment to work on and they know how to do it." The realities in this manager's organization are (not surprisingly) quite different from his pronouncements. His organization is a labyrinth of fiefdoms, turf wars, nonporous organizational boundaries, suspicion, and destructive competition.

This manager's attitude toward facilitators is caused by arrogance, i.e., the inability to admit to the need for help. My conversations with him have led me to conclude that he thinks that, if he were to utilize facilitators (and team training), he would be admitting that his organization is not actually a team. His reaction reminds me of a similar experience that I had years ago when I was offering a productivity-improvement seminar for a client. The managers who attended the seminar took issue with the topic on the grounds that it implied that they were not already productive.

Team Competencies for Facilitating

A final team characteristic that determines the need for a designated facilitator is the competence that the team has for facilitating its own meetings. This competence is a function of training, experience, and discipline.

How can a team develop the competence to manage its own facilitation? It can employ the following:

1. **The Model for Successful Team Meetings.** This model (Figure 2-2) presents a comprehensive description of the primary variables that must be managed to ensure that meetings are successful. The model can serve as an introduction to the various actions that a team must take to ensure success. The model can be used to evaluate a team's meetings and it can be used to troubleshoot the causes of problems in meetings, whenever they occur. Finally, the model can help team members to develop a common understanding about the kind of meeting they are trying to create. All in all, the model promotes unity and clarity of purpose. It helps members to visualize what they are doing and gives them a common framework within which they can manage their meetings collaboratively.

2. **Training.** A second action that teams can take is to train each of their members in the skills of team-managed facilitation. This book is the principal resource for such training.

3. **Rotating the Role.** Facilitation requires practice. The easiest way for team members to obtain such practice is to rotate the role of designated facilitator among all members. The learning and skill development that can be achieved through such rotation is enhanced if it is coupled with feedback from the team. Feedback can be oral or written. Regardless of the form that is used, feedback should be brief and concrete. An example of a feedback form is found in Figure 2-4.

4. **Self-Evaluation.** A final way that a team can improve its competence in facilitating its own meetings is to evaluate itself. The Team-Managed-Facilitation Evaluation Form (Figure 2-3) assesses the team's performance during a meeting using the variables included in the Model for Successful Team Meetings. The assumption is that, if a team scores high on this evaluation, it has had a successful meeting and must have carried out its facilitation role satisfactorily.

THE GOALS OF FACILITATION

In the introduction to this book, I suggested that the general purpose of facilitation is to make things easy. If we couple this description with the three criteria for successful team meetings, we can list the goals of facilitation as making it easy for teams:

1. To perform their tasks;
2. To develop as teams; and
3. To improve their meetings.

The foundation goal is improving meetings. It is by improving meetings that teams can advance with certainty toward the other two goals.

INTERVENTIONS

The purpose of facilitation is to help the team to succeed. The facilitation of any team meeting is successful if it, in turn, helps the team to meet the three goals listed previously. Meeting these goals is the measure of a team's success. Meeting these goals also becomes the criteria for measuring the success of the facilitation and the facilitator. Facilitation has been successful if:

- The team achieves its tasks in a highly efficient way, i.e., team members experience little or no waste in time or other resources;
- The team develops further as a team, i.e., the strength of commitment, loyalty, collaboration, etc., are improved; and
- The team's meetings improve and support more fully the team's development as a team and its task performance.

An intervention is any statement or action made by anyone during a meeting that helps the team to perform a task or subtask and to reach its goals. Interventions may be made by a designated facilitator or by anyone else who is participating in a team meeting. The more competent a team becomes in managing its own facilitation, the more interventions will be made by members.

Interventions can take the form of suggestions, observations, the use of structured problem-solving tools, feedback, and so on. As facilitation is described in this book, guidance for the kind of interventions that are made comes from the Model for Successful Team Meetings (Figure 2-2).

Improving team development and improving task performance are based on improving the shape and process of the team meeting. This position assumes the following:

- That the facilitator is operating from a model of what a successful team meeting looks like; and
- That this model integrates the notion of a successful meeting with task performance and team development.

The Model for Successful Team Meetings, which will be fully described in Chapter 2, provides a way to conceptualize the functions of facilitation and a rationale for selecting and using specific interventions that ensure team development and successful task performance.

SUMMARY OF CHAPTER'S KEY POINTS

The key learning points for this chapter are:

1. All teams meet—some often and some infrequently. Each team meeting is a potential opportunity for improvement.

2. Teams perform many tasks and subtasks. One key function of facilitation is to help the team to identify concretely what tasks it intends to complete and the various subtasks that are associated with that task.

3. All teams can benefit from disciplined facilitation. The need for a designated facilitator does not depend on the kind of team involved. The need for a designated facilitator depends on: (1) the level of development of the team and its capacity to manage its own facilitation; (2) the level of difficulty of the tasks that the team is undertaking; and (3) the competencies that the team has for facilitating its own meetings.

4. Team meetings differ greatly from team to team. All team meetings, however, have three things in common. They always: (1) present an opportunity to perform a task; (2) present an opportunity for the team to develop itself as a team; and (3) present an opportunity for improving present and future team meetings.

5. The general purpose of facilitation is to make things easier. The following goals become the criteria for successful team meetings: (1) perform the tasks; (2) develop as a team; and (3) improve the team's meetings. The foundation criterion is improving meetings. It is by improving meetings that the other two criteria are met. Successful facilitation consists of helping teams to improve their meetings.

6. Interventions may be made by a designated facilitator or by anyone else who is participating in a team meeting. The more competent a team becomes in managing its own facilitation, the more interventions

will be made by members. Interventions may take the form of suggestions, observations, the use of structured problem-solving tools, feedback, etc. As facilitation is described in this book, guidance for the kinds of interventions that are made comes from the Model for Successful Team Meetings (Figure 2-2).

Chapter 2

The Foundation: A Model for Successful Team Meetings

Teams need to have meetings in order to carry out a multitude of functions that relate to their formation, development, and performance. Meetings are not (or at least should not be) ends in themselves. They are held so that team members can share information and ideas, set goals, make decisions, solve problems, evaluate their performance, and design and implement specific improvement projects. Improvement projects may focus on the team's own development or on its output and customer satisfaction, processes, or input and supplier performance (Kinlaw, 1992).

The primary purpose of facilitation is to assist teams to conduct successful team meetings. The various functions and subfunctions of facilitation derive from this purpose. The critical competence required for facilitation is an understanding of the variables that are key to successful team meetings and how these variables are related. In short, facilitation is based on a model of successful team meetings that defines all the functions of facilitation and the typical interventions that are required. *The foundation for facilitation and facilitator skills is the Model for Successful Team Meetings.*

The Model for Successful Team Meetings is *not* a complete model of facilitation; a complete description of facilitation would include a lot more information than that which can be contained in the model. However, the model is a primary tool for facilitation; it establishes the foundation of facilitation by focusing facilitation on the *conditions* that *determine the success* of a team meeting. The model is a framework for organizing the purposes of facilitation and guiding the choice of interventions.

The specific interventions required in facilitation and the specific competencies associated with facilitation must be fully congruent with the model. There are, no doubt, countless possible interventions that might be made at any given time during a meeting that will be useful. Any intervention is useful so long as it is based on an accurate diagnosis of which of the variables identified in the model requires support.

In the following chapters, detailed information is presented about how the Model for Successful Team Meetings can be used to anticipate the kinds of interventions that will be required in facilitating a successful meeting and how the model can be used to help team members and designated facilitators diagnose the needs of a team during a meeting and make the appropriate intervention.

This chapter presents the Model for Successful Team Meetings and gives an overview of the model's major components. In later chapters, each of these components will be discussed in detail and related to the facilitator's function in helping the team to strengthen that component. Also in later chapters, specific interventions are classified, and specific facilitator skills are described and illustrated.

ORIGINS OF THE MODEL

Most people in organizations already spend a considerable amount of time in meetings. Indications are that they will spend more and more time in such meetings. The core organizational management functions of planning, organizing, staffing, implementing, and evaluating all are accomplished in meetings. Meetings also are an integral part of almost every work sequence or process, such as producing designs and drawings, preparing budgets, testing systems, maintaining equipment, etc. As far back as 1987, one study suggested that the average manager and technical professional spent about one-fourth of their time in meetings (Mosvick & Nelson, 1987).

Teams have long been recognized as the fundamental units of performance. More and more, they are recognized as the fundamental source for the continuous improvement of quality. The general acceptance of total quality management as the key to sustained superior performance has resulted in a massive movement toward team formation and team development in organizations. This movement has resulted in a quantum leap in the frequency of meetings for teams to plan work, solve problems, and undertake projects in continuous improvement.

There is no shortage of meetings, and there is no lack of people who have lengthy experience in participating in meetings. These people are an enormous source of information about meetings—what makes them work and what keeps them from working.

One of the major sources for the Model for Successful Meetings has been the many hundreds of people whom I have asked to participate in the following exercise:

1. Think about a small group meeting in which you have recently participated that did not go as well as it might have—was not as efficient or as effective as it might have been.

2. Now think of the various blocks or hindrances that kept the meeting from being more successful.

Some of the typical responses that I have collected from people are:

1. People did not do their homework. They were not prepared.

2. We did not have the right people at the meeting. Some people had nothing to lose.

3. There was not enough time to finish the task.

4. The space we had was so small that I was uncomfortable during the whole meeting.

5. We did not have the support we needed from upper management.

6. There was no agenda.

7. We did not know exactly what we were supposed to do.

8. People kept straggling in after we had started.

9. I was never sure how we would make our decisions.

10. I could never figure out if there was a plan for the meeting.

11. We never seemed to follow a set sequence or logic.

12. Everything was confused; it was hard to tell where we were going.

13. We just started talking about the problem without figuring out how we should go about the whole thing.

14. We kept getting off on all kinds of unrelated topics.

15. We kept jumping around and forgetting what we had done or where we were going.

16. Everyone talked at once, and nobody listened.

17. A few people just monopolized the conversation.

18. People were so concerned about their own ideas that no one bothered to find out other people's ideas.

19. We spent most of the time just arguing.

20. People were afraid to say what they really thought.

21. People were too anxious to solve problems before they really understood them.

22. We did not ask enough questions.

23. Too often, we accepted the opinions of the people who had the most authority.

24. We over-simplified the problem. It was a lot more complex than we recognized.

25. We were too willing to go for the most obvious answer.

In analyzing these responses (and hundreds more like them), I have found that they tend to fall into five categories. The numbers in parentheses refer to the examples above.

1. lack of **resources** (1-5);

2. inadequate **structure** (6-10);

3. failure to use **rational processes** (11-15);

4. poor quality of **communication** (16-20); and

5. failure to develop a clear **understanding** of the task, problem, decision, etc. (21-25).

In a survey of 950 managers and technical professionals, Mosvick and Nelson (1987) obtained results that support the accuracy of the five categories that I have identified. Their list of the top sixteen problems in meetings (in order of importance) is as follows:

- getting off the subject;
- no goals or agenda;
- too lengthy;
- poor or inadequate preparation;
- inconclusive;
- disorganized;
- ineffective leadership/lack of control;
- irrelevance of information discussed;
- time wasted during meetings;
- starting late;
- not effective for making decisions;
- interruptions from within and without;
- individuals dominate/aggrandize discussion;
- rambling, redundant, or digressive discussion;
- no published results or follow-up actions; and
- no premeeting orientation/canceled or postponed meetings.

Each of these problems can be placed in one or more of the five categories that I have identified. These categories form the primary elements in the Model for Successful Team Meetings.

THE MODEL FOR SUCCESSFUL TEAM MEETINGS

The Model for Successful Team Meetings has been in the process of development for twenty years. Over that time, I have collected hundreds of responses similar to those listed in the section above. I have had the opportunity to test various versions of the model in various developmental initiatives that I have undertaken with all sorts of teams. I also have used variations of the model in a number of studies about team performance and to design training programs related to team meetings, team facilitation, team membership, and team leadership. Finally, I have used the model to design various team-assessment instruments.

I published a form of the model in my book, *Developing Superior Work Teams: Building Quality and the Competitive Edge* (1991). Since that time, I have had the opportunity to test further the utility and accuracy of the model through extensive involvement in forming and developing teams for total quality management.

Team meetings must be judged by the results they produce. A successful team meeting is one in which:

1. All tasks have been performed effectively and efficiently;

2. The team has achieved its tasks such that it has further developed itself as a team and ensured its capacity to continue to produce excellent results in the future; and

3. The team meeting is consciously viewed as an object of continuous improvement.

The *results* that a team produces depend on the *potential* that it brings to its meeting and the *performance* that it demonstrates during its meeting. A fully successful team meeting occurs when a team maximizes its potential and then maximizes the use that it makes of this potential by the way that it performs during the meeting. The relationship between potential, performance, and results is shown in Figure 2-1.

The *potential* of a team is composed of its assets, i.e., what it has developed before it actually begins to interact and conduct its meeting. Potential is made up of two subelements: *resources* and *structures*.

The *performance* of a team during a meeting largely is a function of how well its members *communicate;* how well it uses *rational processes* to conduct its meeting, make decisions, and solve problems; and how well it develops *understanding* of its tasks, i.e., issues to be resolved, problems to be solved, decisions to be made.

The key variables that determine the success of a team meeting are resources, structures, communication, rational processes, and understanding. These variables and their relationships make up the Model for Successful Team Meetings displayed in Figure 2-2.

The Model and Core Facilitation Competencies

The model describes what must exist in order for a team to make the very most of a meeting, i.e., reach the three key *results* of: (1) task performance, (2) team development, and (3) improvement of its current and future meetings. *Resources* and *structures* must be attended to and managed.

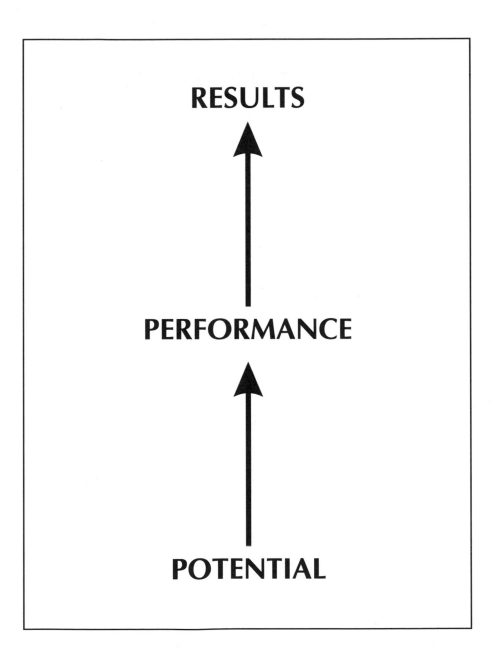

RESULTS

PERFORMANCE

POTENTIAL

Figure 2-1: Key Elements in Successful Meetings

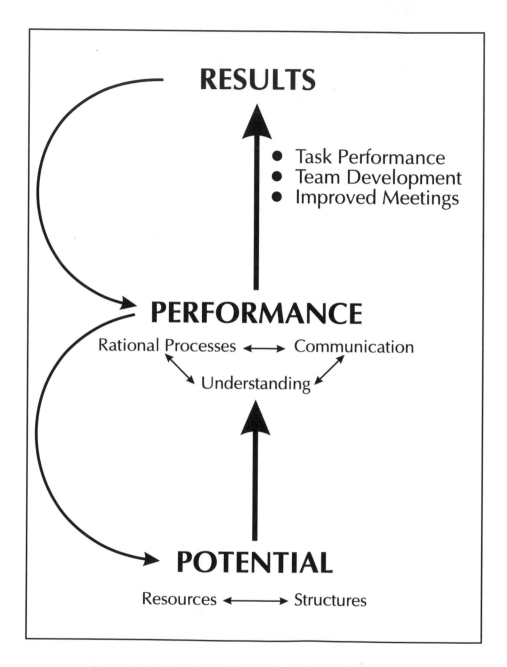

RESULTS

- Task Performance
- Team Development
- Improved Meetings

PERFORMANCE

Rational Processes ⟷ Communication

Understanding

POTENTIAL

Resources ⟷ Structures

Figure 2-2: The Model for Successful Team Meetings

The team must follow *rational processes*. Team members must interact with quality communication and they must develop information and explore alternatives until their decisions reflect a full *understanding* of their task.

These variables, when taken in aggregate, constitute the sufficient conditions for successful team meetings. The purpose of facilitation is to make it easy for teams to create these variables during their meetings. The variables are prepotent. Results depend on performance and potential. Performance depends on potential.

The development of the variables in the model results from team members and designated facilitators making interventions during a meeting to help the reality of the meeting correspond to the design projected in the model. These interventions, in turn, depend on the adequate use of four sets of core facilitative competencies. Figure 2-3 shows the relationship between the model's variables and these core competencies.

The logic expressed in Figure 2-3 is that the development and deployment of a team's potential and its real-time performance are facilitated when interventions are based on:

- Using the model,
- Keeping the team conscious,
- Modeling quality communication, and
- Listening to understand.

These core competencies are fully illustrated in Chapter 3 and are described in detail in Chapter 4. In the sections that follow in this chapter, each of the variables defined in the model is discussed and clarified.

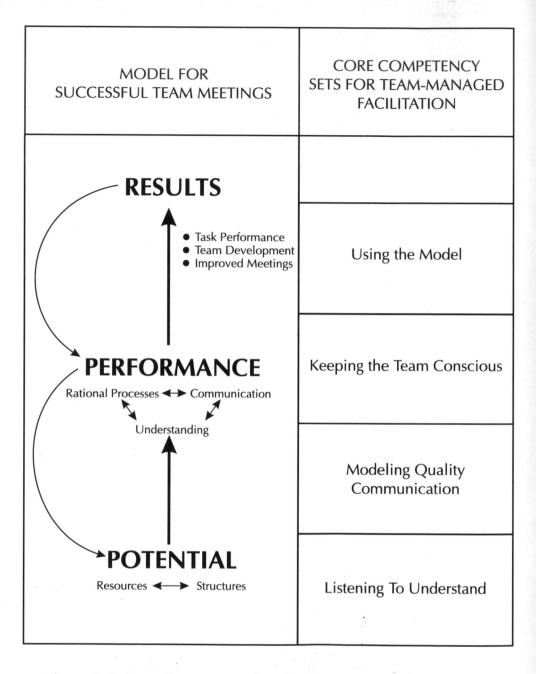

MODEL FOR SUCCESSFUL TEAM MEETINGS	CORE COMPETENCY SETS FOR TEAM-MANAGED FACILITATION
RESULTS • Task Performance • Team Development • Improved Meetings	Using the Model
PERFORMANCE Rational Processes ◄► Communication Understanding	Keeping the Team Conscious
	Modeling Quality Communication
POTENTIAL Resources ◄► Structures	Listening To Understand

Figure 2-3: Core-Competency Sets for Team-Managed Facilitation

POTENTIAL

Teams can produce only the results that they have the potential to produce. A major function of facilitation is to help teams to increase their potential.

Members and designated facilitators can improve the potential of a team by helping the team to strengthen its resources and/or to develop appropriate structures.

Resources

Resources can be strengthened by helping teams to improve what they already have and identify what they need to get. Examples of team resources that impact the success of team meetings are:

- The right people are at the meeting;
- Members are committed to the purposes of the team meeting and the value of the meeting;
- Members have fulfilled all their responsibilities in preparation for the meeting;
- Everyone has access to the information required to achieve the purposes of the meeting;
- Adequate facilities and equipment are available for the meeting;
- The necessary time has been set aside to conduct the meeting;
- The necessary financial resources are available to support the work of the team;
- Members have good communication skills;
- Members have good problem-solving skills; and

- Members have the skills to engage in team-managed facilitation.

Structures

Structures must not be confused with formality. Teams are least likely to be successful if they burden themselves with protocols and strict "rules of order." Structuring means to do everything necessary to ensure that a team is able to take full advantage of its resources. It means to make explicit everything that team members need to know in order to act with full responsibility in the team. Structuring means to do whatever is needed to help the team to avoid communicating and interacting in a random and irrational way. The job of the facilitator is to help the team to identify and resolve questions about roles, goals, norms, decision making, and processes. Examples of such questions are as follows:

Roles:

- Will there be a leader during the meeting?
- What is the leader's job?
- What is expected of each member?
- What are the roles of experts?
- Is the role of the more senior members different from that of the more junior ones?

Norms:

- When will the team meet, start, and finish?
- Will the team start on time and end on time?
- Will it start without everyone being present?

Decision Making:

- How will decisions be made? By voting? By consensus?
- Is the team ready to make a decision?
- Is everyone on the team prepared to support the decision?

Goals:

- What is the purpose of the team?
- What will it accomplish in the present meeting?
- What are the specific results that it is trying to achieve?

Processes:

- What steps will the team follow in answering a question, resolving an issue, or solving a problem?
- What rational problem-solving tool will a team use and how will it use it?
- Will the team evaluate its performance at meetings?
- How and when will it evaluate its performance?

PERFORMANCE

Resources and structures make up the potential that a team has and builds to conduct a superior meeting. The actual results of the meeting are a function of potential and the performance demonstrated during the meeting. There are three elements that interact to produce performance. These are rational processes, communication, and understanding. The facilitator's job is to help team members to use rational processes, reach high levels of interpersonal communication, and develop a thorough understanding of all the tasks and goals that they set out to accomplish.

Rational Processes

Rational processes refer to the flow or sequence by which a team conducts its meetings or any aspect of its meetings. Process refers to the total flow or sequence of an entire meeting as well as various subsequences that take place during a meeting. For example, a team may have decided to use a general problem-solving process that includes the following steps:

1. Define the problem;
2. Develop a strategy for analyzing the problem;
3. Collect and analyze information;
4. Generate possible solutions;
5. Evaluate solutions and select one;
6. Plan action steps, accountability, and measurement systems.

Within this larger process, however, there may be a multitude of subprocesses or routines. The team, for example, may use a cause-and-effect diagram to define the problem. To develop such a diagram, the team must follow a certain rational process. In generating possible solutions, a team might use the nominal group technique or construct a Pareto diagram. All these problem-solving tools follow rational processes.

The facilitator's job is to help the team to identify the process that it is in and then to follow the stages or steps that are associated with the process. The facilitator will help the team to understand what it is doing and then intervene as needed when the team loses consciousness of where it is in the process or begins to abort the process.

Rational processes are closely related to structures. The distinction between the two is that structure refers to the more or less permanent shape of the meeting that is established by norms, role clarification, and how decisions will be made. Rational processes, by contrast, refer to the steps that the team consciously follows in accomplishing its tasks, e.g., following agreed-on steps for brainstorming or staying with one issue without switching unconsciously to another.

Communication

The ways in which team members communicate determines, in large measure, how well they are able to take advantage of their potential. Communication during a team meeting has the greatest utility when it serves any or all of the following functions:

1. Supports the development and use of resources;
2. Supports the development and use of structures;
3. Supports the development and use of rational processes;
4. Keeps the team conscious of what it is doing; and
5. Helps the team to understand and accomplish its intermediate and final tasks and reach its goals.

Communication during a team meeting will tend to serve these functions when what members say is:

- **Appropriate**. Being both timely and relevant to what the team is trying to achieve.

- **Concrete**. Being accurate, being specific, using data, and giving examples.
- **Respectful**. Listening to what others say and trying to use what they say.
- **Team-centered**. Focusing on what the team wants to accomplish rather than on what "I" want to accomplish. Serving the team's needs rather than personal needs.

Team performance during a meeting depends on the ability of team members to use rational processes. It further depends on the ability of team members to communicate in ways that carry out the functions and have the qualities listed above. A third element that determines performance is understanding tasks.

Understanding

The Model for Successful Team Meetings (Figure 2-2) shows the three performance elements of rational processes, communication, and understanding. These are very interdependent; what happens with one element will influence the other elements.

The quality of communication affects how well rational processes are identified and used. How well rational processes are used affects the quality of communication. Both rational processes and communication affect the degree to which teams are able to understand their tasks.

Understanding is created by information, opinions, and questions. It is created by restating what has been said and by summarizing what has been said. It also is created by helping the team members to communicate more concretely and specifically.

RESULTS

Success in the Model for Successful Team Meetings is defined by the results that are achieved. Typically, we think of success in terms of performing the tasks that the team set out to perform. The model, however, suggests that meetings also should achieve two other outcomes, regardless of the specific tasks at hand. The three results that should characterize successful team meetings are:

- Performance of tasks;
- Further development as a team; and
- Improvement of team meetings.

Task Performance

Results are achieved by taking care of the other elements in the model. Results are indirect outcomes. This clearly is the case with task achievement. The degree to which teams manage their resources, structures, rational processes, communication, and understanding will determine the quality of the tasks they achieve. Results, in the model, are a function of *potential* and *performance*. Management of each of the five elements impacts the achievement of tasks in quite specific ways.

Clarity about the tasks to be performed is fundamental to success. Clarification is, first of all, a function of *structures*. It must be addressed *before* the team begins to perform, i.e., interact to make a decision, solve a problem, etc. Tasks also be must defined so that specific *resources* can be obtained. The availability of resources, in turn, will determine the way in which tasks are defined.

Without clarity about tasks, the potential of the team cannot be developed properly. But clarifying tasks is a continuing requirement. It must be accomplished over and over again as teams engage in performing the real work of their meetings. Clarity is achieved by adhering to *rational processes;* practicing high quality *communication* that is appropriate, concrete, respectful, and team-centered; and ensuring that *understanding* has been created through the full development of relevant information.

Building clarity about the tasks to be performed often can be a very time-consuming and difficult task for a team. I recently was involved with a team that was tasked to improve the process for designing and deploying heat, ventilation, and air conditioning controls. The team represented one governmental organization and five different government contractors. It took five, two-hour meetings to determine that the purpose of the team was to: "reduce the cost and improve the quality in the design, procurement, operation, and maintenance of all controls."

Team Development

Team meetings exist first and last for the purpose of performing tasks such as achieving specified goals, solving problems, making decisions, and designing improvement projects. They also should be viewed as one of several opportunities for developing the team.

Team development is the process of maturing into a superior team. There are four sets of characteristics that distinguish superior teams and which any team can use to rate team development and identify improvement opportunities (Kinlaw, 1991). These are:

1. **Team Results.** Superior teams consistently achieve the following: maximum use of its people; delivery of superior services and products in the face of every conceivable difficulty; continuous improvement; and enthusiastically positive customers.

2. **Informal Processes**. Superior teams create and make extensive use of informal processes such as: communicating and contacting; responding and adapting; influencing and improving; and appreciating and celebrating.

3. **Positive Team Feelings**. Members of superior teams typically share feelings of: inclusion, commitment, loyalty, pride, and trust.

4. **Leadership**. Among the special roles that superior team leaders fulfill are initiator, model, and coach.

Team meetings are, to some degree, ends in themselves; certain tasks are actually achieved and real work is done. But team meetings also can be means to a greater end. They can serve to strengthen the capacity of a team to be a superior team in every aspect of its performance.

For example, we know that superior teams are characterized by team members having strong feelings of inclusion. Team meetings support the development of this feeling to the degree that every team member participates fully at meetings, the ideas of every member are taken seriously and fully explored, no one dominates, and everyone feels free to be candid and honest.

Improved Meetings

A third result of successful team meetings is that each meeting serves to improve the competencies of team members to manage their own meetings. This result, like team development, easily can be overlooked in a team's haste to get on with its agenda and perform its tasks.

Team meetings must be viewed as real team work. They must be seen, not as necessary evils, but as critical to a team's success as any other operation in the multitude of work processes in which teams are involved.

Improving meetings is an obvious target for continuous improvement in most organizations. Meetings always are listed among the top one or two time wasters by key employees. Most meetings waste time, money, and human resources.

The Model for Successful Team Meetings makes the improvement of team meetings an explicit expected result. Teams should set out to meet in order that they can improve the way in which they meet. The primary function of the model and of team-managed facilitation is to ensure that this result is achieved. The model provides a benchmark for what the very best team meetings look like. Regular evaluation of the performance of teams during their meetings provides baselines for measuring how well team meetings are being managed and helps teams to identify new targets of opportunity.

USES OF THE MODEL

The uses to which a team or designated facilitator will put the Model for Successful Team Meetings are:

1. To provide team members and facilitators at the front end of a team meeting with a way to conceptualize and become sensitive to the kinds of interventions that may be required to help a team create the

conditions for a successful meeting, e.g., interventions that help the team to use its resources, create structure, employ rational processes, practice quality communication, and build understanding.

2. To provide a conceptual basis for identifying the general competencies that will be needed for facilitation, e.g., team members and designated facilitators must be able to help the team to structure itself, identify and use its resources, use rational processes, etc.

3. To provide team members and designated facilitators *at the back end* of a team meeting with a framework for evaluating the performance of the team or the performance of the designated facilitator. Use of the model stimulates such questions as "Were interventions made to help the team use its resources, create structure, employ rational processes, practice quality communication, and build understanding?"

4. To give team members and facilitators a basic tool for facilitating the real-time performance of their meetings by giving them a framework with which they can accurately identify what the team needs to do to help move itself toward achieving successful outcomes. By constant mental reference to the model, team members and designated facilitators will identify what issue must be addressed. Is it that the team is not following a sequence that it previously agreed to follow? Is it that the team is no longer following its norms?

In the following chapters, I provide a full description of how the model is used in facilitation. The following is an overview of the various ways in which the model is used.

Front-End Conceptual Framework

The model provides the team with a precise view of the variables that it must manage. The model is used as the blueprint for each meeting. The model functions as a set of quality standards within which the team functions. The function of facilitation is to take those actions (i.e., perform those interventions) that can help the team to bring itself into compliance with these standards. Each time the team is not managing any of the key elements properly (i.e., its structures, resources, rational processes, communication, and understanding), the function of facilitation is to help the team to do so.

Competencies for Facilitation

The competencies required for facilitation are to help the team to:

- Structure itself by clarifying desired outcomes, norms, roles, agenda, sequences, and processes;
- Identify the resources it needs and the resources it has and use these resources fully;
- Select the rational processes for performing its tasks (developing information, solving problems, learning, making decisions, designing improvement projects, etc.) and stay conscious of how it is using these processes; and
- Communicate in real time to achieve its tasks.

The competencies required for team-managed facilitation will be discussed in detail in Chapter 4.

A Back-End Framework for Evaluation

The model is a baseline. Teams can use the model to evaluate their performance at any time. Such evaluation can be done directly from the model, by reviewing each of the elements and discussing how well each of these elements was managed. Or the team may use an evaluation form such as the one in Figure 2-4. This form covers the six elements in the model. It can be used at the end of a meeting or at the end of a major activity carried out at a meeting.

The Team-Managed-Facilitation Evaluation Form should be used in the following way:

1. The team reviews the form and makes certain that everyone understands each item.

2. The team agrees on how the form will be used and when it will be used.

3. Each team member completes the form. Results are summarized and displayed to the whole team.

4. The team identifies opportunities for improvement and how to make the improvements.

5. Improvements are planned and implemented. The form is completed at intervals, and the results are summarized and tracked.

The model should not be used only to evaluate the team's total performance during a meeting; it should be used to evaluate the facilitation of the meeting. There are two opportunities for evaluating team-managed facilitation. The first opportunity is in regard to the performance

5 = Fully agree   1 = Do not agree at all

1. We used everyone as a resource.   5 4 3 2 1

2. We used our time effectively.   5 4 3 2 1

3. We made good use of the information   5 4 3 2 1
   available to us.

4. We adhered to our team-meeting norms.   5 4 3 2 1

5. We remained clear about our tasks.   5 4 3 2 1

6. We remained clear about our   5 4 3 2 1
   responsibilities.

7. We clarified the steps we would follow   5 4 3 2 1
   in performing our tasks.

8. We stayed conscious of the processes   5 4 3 2 1
   that we were trying to use.

9. We quickly got back on track when we   5 4 3 2 1
   became confused.

10. We kept our inputs relevant.   5 4 3 2 1

11. We kept our inputs concrete.   5 4 3 2 1

12. We communicated respectfully with   5 4 3 2 1
    one another.

13. We developed sufficient information   5 4 3 2 1
    about all topics discussed.

14. We explored alternatives fully before   5 4 3 2 1
    making decisions.

15. We encouraged differences in opinion.   5 4 3 2 1

Figure 2-4: Team-Managed-Facilitation Evaluation Form

Team-Managed Facilitation

of all team members as facilitators. Teams are responsible for their own facilitation and must periodically evaluate the team's total performance in facilitation. The second opportunity for evaluation is the performance of the designated facilitator.

My experience in most training programs that are called "facilitator training" is that they provide no basis by which to define and determine success. The great majority of such programs do not (at the outset) define exactly what constitutes successful facilitation and they provide feedback on the performance of trainees that is completely lacking in rigor and concrete specification. No one fails in such training because there are no standards or limits.

Some years ago, I became interested in trying to introduce precision into the process of training people in various processes of interpersonal communication. It is nonsense to run training programs in which there are no standards, especially when we know what the standards are. There are some clear, proven rules that must be obeyed in conversations between two people who are mutually trying to solve some problem. There also are rules that must be obeyed when one person confronts another and expects that there will be a positive outcome. I have included some of these rules in my book, *Coaching for Commitment: Managerial Strategies for Obtaining Superior Performance* (Kinlaw, 1989).

The model provides a very clear basis for assessing the performance of facilitators—whether designated or not. The assessment of facilitation—like everything else in team-managed facilitation—depends on the model. The model suggests the following kinds of questions for facilitation and facilitators:

- Were your interventions clearly supportive of the team reaching its goals of task performance, team development, and improved team meetings?
- Did your interventions help the team to: (1) identify and use its resources? (2) develop and use the necessary structures for conducting its meeting? (3) develop and use the necessary rational processes for doing its business? (4) communicate in ways that were appropriate, concrete, respectful, and team centered? (5) develop full understanding of the topic, issue, or problem?
- Did you keep the team conscious at all times of what it was doing?
- Did you model good communication behaviors throughout the meeting?

Figure 2-5 is a Designated-Facilitator Evaluation Form that can be used to give feedback to a designated facilitator. However, it also can be adapted and used by a team to evaluate the whole team's demonstrated skills in facilitating its own meeting.

This form, or any other such evaluation tool, should be used to identify opportunities for improvement, not to identify shortcomings and failures.

A Framework for Interventions

Facilitation is accomplished by making an appropriate intervention. In the view of facilitation presented in this book, these interventions always will address one or more problems related to the key elements.

5 = Fully agree   1 = Do not agree at all

The designated facilitator helped us to:

1. Use everyone as a resource.   5 4 3 2 1

2. Use our time effectively.   5 4 3 2 1

3. Make good use of the information   5 4 3 2 1
    available to us.

4. Adhere to our team-meeting norms.   5 4 3 2 1

5. Remain clear about our tasks.   5 4 3 2 1

6. Remain clear about our responsibilities.   5 4 3 2 1

7. Clarify the steps we would follow in   5 4 3 2 1
    performing our tasks.

8. Stay conscious of the processes that   5 4 3 2 1
    we were trying to use.

9. Get back on track when we became   5 4 3 2 1
    confused.

10. Keep our inputs relevant.   5 4 3 2 1

11. Keep our inputs concrete.   5 4 3 2 1

12. Communicate respectfully with one   5 4 3 2 1
    another.

13. Develop sufficient information about   5 4 3 2 1
    all topics discussed.

14. Explore alternatives fully before making   5 4 3 2 1
    decisions.

15. Encourage differences in opinion.   5 4 3 2 1

Figure 2-5: Designated-Facilitator Evaluation Form

Anyone who acts as facilitator at any moment during a team's meeting performs the following sequence in reasoning:

1. Some problem or opportunity for improvement is observed. For example, communication may be confused, random, or unfocused.

2. The facilitator relates the problem to one or more of the key elements by asking the question, "Is this problem one of resources, structures, rational process, communication, or understanding?"

3. The facilitator shares with the team what the facilitator has observed and is thinking.

4. The team, with the help of the facilitator, decides what should be done. For example, if the team has lost its focus, it may be because the goal or task is no longer clear, or it may be that the sequence of the process is not being followed.

The Model and the Logic of Facilitation

In describing the Model for Successful Team Meetings, I have emphasized that the model is not a model of facilitation; it is a model of what a successful meeting looks like. The model is a tool for facilitation—albeit the primary tool. Facilitation derives its shape from the model. We can infer from the model the kinds of interventions that will facilitate a team meeting and we can infer the kinds of competencies that will be required to make such interventions.

A full understanding of team-managed facilitation includes the following layers of logic:

1. First, we understand that all team members are responsible to facilitate the cooperative generation of a successful meeting. The precise meaning of success is described by the Model for Successful Team Meetings. The model defines the criteria for success and the variables that determine success.

2. Second, we derive from the key variables in the model what kind of facilitative interventions will be required. Team members and designated facilitators will be required to make interventions to build structure, use resources, follow rational processes, etc.

3. Third, in order to make the kinds of interventions that are required, team members and designated facilitators must have a minimum set of key competencies. These competencies are illustrated in Chapter 3 and are discussed in detail in Chapter 4. A summary of these sets of competencies is:

   - Using the model,
   - Keeping the team conscious,
   - Modeling quality communication, and
   - Listening to understand.

SUMMARY OF CHAPTER'S KEY POINTS

In this chapter, I have covered the following topics:

- The Model for Successful Team Meetings and its key elements; and
- Uses of the Model for Successful Team Meetings.

The key points covered in this chapter are:

1. The primary role in facilitation is to assist teams to achieve the results of: task performance, team development, and improved meetings.

2. The foundation for facilitation and facilitator skills is the Model for Successful Team Meetings.

3. The key elements that teams must manage in order to achieve successful results are resources, structures, rational processes, communication, and understanding.

4. Resources can be strengthened by helping teams to improve what they already have and identify what they need to get.

5. Structuring can be strengthened by helping teams be explicit about what members must do to act with full responsibility in the team. Structuring means to do whatever is needed to help the team to avoid communicating and interacting in a random and irrational way.

6. Rational processes are strengthened when facilitators: (1) help the team to identify the process that it is in and then to follow the stages or steps that are associated with the process; (2) help the team to understand what it is doing and then intervene as needed when the team loses consciousness of where it is in the process or begins to abort the process.

7. Communication is strengthened by helping team members to speak so that what they say is:

- **Appropriate**. Being both timely and relevant to what the team is trying to achieve.

- **Concrete**. Being accurate, being specific, using data, and giving examples.

- **Respectful**. Listening to what others say and trying to use what they say.

- **Team-centered**. Focusing on what the team wants to accomplish rather than on what "I" want to accomplish. Serving the team's needs rather than personal needs.

8. Understanding of goals, purposes, and tasks is created largely through developing information.

9. The uses to which team members and their designated facilitators will put the Model for Successful Team Meetings are:

- To provide team members and facilitators at the front end of a team meeting with a way to conceptualize and become sensitive to the kinds of interventions that may be required to help a team create the conditions for a successful meeting, e.g., interventions that help the team to use its resources, create structure, employ rational processes, practice quality communication, and build understanding.

- To provide a conceptual basis for identifying the general competencies that will be needed for facilitation, e.g., team members and designated facilitators must be able to help the team to structure itself, identify and use its resources, use rational processes, etc.

- To provide team members and designated facilitators *at the back end* of a team meeting with a framework for evaluating the performance of the team or the performance of the designated facilitator. Use of the model stimulates such questions as "Were interventions made to help the team use its resources, create structure, employ rational processes, practice quality communication, and build understanding?"

- To give team members and facilitators a basic tool for facilitating the real-time performance of their meetings by giving them a framework with which they can accurately identify what the team needs to do to help move itself toward achieving successful outcomes. By constant mental reference to the model, team members and designated facilitators will identify what issue must be addressed. Is it that the team is not following a sequence that it previously agreed to follow? Is it that the team is no longer following its norms?

In the next chapter, we will look at facilitation in action. I will demonstrate what team-managed facilitation is with a brief dramatization of a meeting. We will see what we can expect a team meeting to look like when a team uses the Model for Successful Team Meetings and its members work at using the skills of team-managed facilitation.

Chapter 3

Team-Managed
Facilitation in Practice:
A Behavioral Dramatization

In the introduction and the first two chapters of this book, I describe team-managed facilitation and how it differs from traditional views of facilitation. I also describe the Model for Successful Team Meetings and state that it is the foundation and framework for facilitating team meetings.

In this chapter, I want to provide a sense of what team facilitation is in actual practice. Rather than just describe it, I will show what it looks like by modeling the kinds of communication behaviors that are characteristic of team-managed facilitation. I do this in the form of a dramatization. The dramatization can be viewed as a summary or synthesis of hundreds of team meetings in which team-managed facilitation has been employed. As you read the behavioral dramatization, note that it emphasizes certain key characteristics of team-managed facilitation. These characteristics are as follows:

1. Team-managed facilitation is empirical, structured, explicit, and rational.

2. Team-managed facilitation may or may not involve a designated facilitator. Even if there is a designated facilitator, the team remains responsible for its own

facilitation, and every team member is responsible for functioning as a facilitator.

3. The key functions of team facilitation are derived from the Model for Successful Team Meetings. These functions are:

   - Support the development and use of resources;
   - Support the development and use of structures;
   - Support the development and use of rational processes;
   - Help the team maintain quality in its communications; and
   - Help the team to understand and achieve its intermediate and final tasks.

4. Some of the kinds of tasks that facilitators help teams to perform are: making decisions, solving problems, sharing information, learning, and designing improvement projects.

5. The goals of facilitation are to help the team: (1) to perform its tasks; (2) to develop as a team; and (3) to improve its meetings.

6. Facilitative interventions are built on the four sets of competencies:

   - Using the model,
   - Keeping the team conscious,
   - Modeling quality communication, and
   - Listening to understand.

This dramatization is a behavioral model. The communication behaviors are intended to be positive examples. Nevertheless, I have used a few nonfacilitative behaviors for the purposes of contrast and instruction.

COMMENTARY NOTES

In the right-hand margin are notes about the comments made by the players in the dramatization. Each note is numbered for easy reference. Following the number, the letters "F" or "NF" appear. F indicates that the input is facilitative. NF indicates that the input is nonfacilitative. After the designation F or NF there is a slash mark. This slash mark is followed by an identification of the element in the model that the input most closely supports, i.e., resources, structures, rational processes, communication, or understanding. These elements are abbreviated in the notes as:

- RES = Resources;
- STR = Structures;
- RAP = Rational Processes;
- COM = Communication; and
- UND = Understanding.

Sometimes the element being supported is followed by a word or phase in parentheses. This word or phrase gives more specific information about the element. For example the note, "1F/STR(Roles)" indicates that the member's input is facilitative, it supports the development of structures, and the kind of structure that it supports is establishing the roles of team members. The note "23F/RAP(Keeping Conscious)" describes the comment of a team member as facilitative and supporting the use of rational processes by helping the team to stay conscious of what it is doing.

Comments from team members often have multiple effects. Also, it is not always possible to make too fine a distinction between resources, structures, processes, communication, and understanding. A note, therefore, may not include all the effects that a specific comment might have. The notes try to draw attention only to the dominant effects that any comment might have. In instances in which two elements of the model are clearly supported by a single input, both these elements are noted. For example, the note "80F/COM(Consensus)/UND" indicates that the input has helped the team to communicate and verify consensus, but the comment also has improved the team's understanding of its task (in this case, by verifying that the special meetings under discussion will be called "team meetings").

SETTING

The Computer Assistance Team (CAT) recently has been reorganized to respond to the increased requirement in the Metacomputing Company for a central computer-service center that has the engineering and technical competence to repair and restore promptly to full operation every aspect of all of its internal computing systems. Metacomputing is fully committed to team formation and development throughout the company. This commitment is expressed in the personal management philosophy of the founder of Metacomputing, Dr. J. Alethos, who was quoted in a recent issue of *The Chronos Journal* as saying:

> Within the next ten years, teamwork will be the dominant way in which organizations do work or they will have no work to do. Team players are the only kind of players we can afford at Metacomputing. We don't

have leaders and we don't have followers. We have team members. We still use the terms "lead," "supervisor," and "manager." But people in these jobs are evaluated on how well they *lead* teams, how good they are at *supervising* teams, and how successful they are in *managing* teams. When you ask people in our company to tell you what jobs they have, we expect them to tell you of which primary work team they are members, of their various process teams, and of any management teams on which they might be serving.

It is a policy at Metacomputing that every person and every team receive team-development training each year. It also is a policy that each new or reorganized organizational component attend two company training programs, "Superior Team Development" and "Team-Managed Facilitation," within two weeks of being organized or reorganized.

CAT members have all gone through the two training programs. The action begins at the first meeting of CAT on a Monday following the Friday on which the team's training was completed.

THE CAST OF PLAYERS

Alex . . . . Designated Facilitator
Claire . . . . Hardware Specialist
Don . . . . CAD/CAM Specialist
John . . . . Software Specialist
Mat . . . . Network Specialist
Kim . . . . Administrative Specialist
Stella . . . . Team Leader

SCENE ONE

[Team members are seated along two small rectangular tables that form a "V." At the open end of the "V" is a flip chart. Standing by the chart is Alex.]

Stella: When we ended the facilitator training last week, we agreed that Alex would serve as the designated facilitator at our first meeting. At the risk of "carrying coals to Newcastle" and repeating the obvious, let's keep in mind that facilitating our meetings is everyone's job. Alex is going to help us. We are going to help Alex. Most of all, we are going to help ourselves. It looks as if everyone has the notebook from our facilitator training course, so I guess we're ready to start. **1F/STR(Norms)**

          2F/RES

Alex: Hear, hear! Yea verily and right on! You all know as much as I do about this sort of thing; just keep in mind that your day in the barrel will come soon enough. **3F/STR (Outcomes)**

This is our first meeting, so I guess we will be doing a number of things that we won't be doing at every meeting. I propose that we start with the same sequence that we learned at facilitator training. We have scheduled two hours for this meeting. One more

item. How does this seating arrange- **4F/RES**
ment suit everyone? Any better way
to arrange ourselves? *[Pauses. Checks
for agreement, then goes to the flip
chart and writes out what follows.]*
First, let's set the norms for our
meeting. Second, let's review the
Model for Superior Team Meetings
so we are all singing the same tune.
Third, I would like to make sure that
we are all agreed about my job as
designated facilitator. Fourth, we
might set some outcomes for this first
meeting. Our fifth item should probably be that we decide how we propose to reach our outcomes today.
Last, but not least, I suggest that we
save time at the end of the meeting
to evaluate our performance with the
Team Evaluation Sheet that we used
during our training last week. How
does this sound to you all?

Mat: I thought we set the norms during **5NF**
the training we just went through.
Why have we got to go through that
again? We could spend the whole
damn meeting getting ready to get
ready to get ready.

Alex: How do the rest of you feel about the **6F/COM**
norms? **(Consensus)**

John: I think we should start from scratch. **7F/UND**
Training is training. This is for real.

Kim: I think that we should at least nail **8F/UND**
down the norms that we are really
going to use, even if we do have to
repeat ourselves a little. If I got anything out of our training, it was just
how important norms are.

Alex: I guess we know how Matthew, John, **9F/COM**
and Kim think. How about the rest of **(Consensus)**
you?

Claire: It will be a whole lot quicker to just **10NF**
do it and not spend the day talking
about it. It won't take us more than
fifteen minutes to brainstorm a set of
norms. We gained some experience
at the training. Let's do it for real.

Don: Fine by me. **11F/COM**
(Agreement)

Stella: I'm for setting our norms now. Looks **12F/COM**
like most of us feel that way, except **(Consensus)**
maybe Mat. How about it, Mat?

Mat: Looks like the rest of you think we **13F/COM**
should set our norms. So, "one more **(Consensus)**
time," let's do it. Just don't think I'm
going to be so easy when we get
down to the serious stuff.

Alex: O.K., so we'll start with norms. Do we need to discuss the other items—review the model, determine the facilitator's role, and so forth—before we start, to see if we are all agreed that these are things we want to do?   **14F/RAP**

Mat: Let's do the norms and then check it out.   **15F/RAP**

Alex: Any objections to that? *[Pauses and waits.]* O.K., I suggest that we use brainstorming and develop a set of norms. I've put the rules for brainstorming on a flip chart. *[Turns chart to rules and reads rules to team.]* Any questions? Let's start.   **16F/COM (Consensus)/STR**

[Lights fade. When they come up again there is a chart on the wall with the heading "CAT Meeting Norms."]

SCENE TWO

[Setting is the same as Scene One. Kim is the first to speak.]

Kim: I propose that we keep the norms posted for at least the next few meetings. Also, I would like to add a norm, and that is that we go over our list at the beginning of each meeting to make sure the list still applies and to see if we need to add something or to emphasize a norm that we may not be keeping too well.   **17F/STR(Norms)**

John: It's O.K. by me to start out the way you say, but I think the process will get really tedious after awhile.   **18NF**

Don: If norms are as important as we keep hearing they are, then we ought to put them to work for us.   **19F/UND**

Mat: In the interest of getting on with whatever work we're going to do, I say let's go with Kim's idea.   **20F/STR/COM (Agreement)**

Claire: If Mat is for it, how can anyone be against it?   **21NF**

Stella: I think we might just add one more thing to what Kim says. I would like to see us use the norms to assess how well we have done at the end of a meeting—at least once a week or so.   **22F/STR**

Mat: Before we all go "norm happy," let me see if I fully understand what we are doing. Are we intending that these norms apply to all the meetings we have? I mean every Monday morning staff meeting, and design-review meetings, and our new TQM meetings?   **23F/UND**

Don: That's how I see it. We're putting norms in place that apply to every meeting we have. And if someone isn't sticking by the norms—in whatever meeting it is—we call the person on it. If we are not going to use the   **24F/STR**

norms and expect one another to stick by them, then what's the purpose of having them?

Alex: Let me jump in here and act like a facilitator. We have sort of branched off from the original issue onto a second one. We were first responding to Kim's suggestion that we review the norms before each meeting to see if they still apply or if they need to be adjusted by adding or deleting some. Claire has proposed that we do what Kim suggests, but that we also use the norms at the end of a meeting to evaluate how we have done. This is the first proposal, then, to review the norms before a meeting and then use them (at intervals) to evaluate our meetings. A second question has been introduced by Mat. His question is whether we intend to use the norms at all our meetings, regardless of the purpose.

25/RAP(Keeping Conscious)

John: I have assumed that our norms will apply to all our meetings. I'm a little surprised at Mat's question. But my answer is "yes."

26F/UND

Claire: Of course it's "yes." Mat, do you have some kind of meeting in mind in which we wouldn't use the norms?

27F/UND

Mat: I don't know. I just see us getting so formal and making so many rules that we might take the fun out of what we do and start acting like a bunch of lawyers. 28F/UND

Stella: I think a way of testing Mat's concern is to look at the norms and ask ourselves if there is any kind of team meeting that we might have in which the norms would not apply. 29F/UND

Mat: I guess what I am really asking is if one or two of us get together to work a problem—you know, when it's not really a team meeting—then what? Do we invoke the norms? 30F/UND

Claire: At the risk of repeating myself, the answer is still "yes." Which of the norms would you not want to use at any meeting among any of us at any time and for any reason? Is it "no nit-picking?" Is it "be concrete?" Is it "treat one another with respect?" Is it "decide by consensus?" I just don't see anything up there *[points to the chart]* that I don't intend to stick by, regardless of the time, place, or purpose of any meeting that I might have with any of you in the future. 31F/UND

Mat: Stella sure knows how she feels about the norms. Is that how the rest of you 32F/COM (Consensus)

feel? Do these things apply to us all the time—whenever we meet?

Kim: I never really thought about it, but I can't see why we wouldn't want the norms to apply all the time.   33F/UND

Alex: Are we ready to settle Mat's question? Do the norms apply to all of our meetings?   34F/COM (Consensus)

John: To take any view other than that the norms apply to all our meetings could lead us into a lot of crazy stuff. We could spend the next week deciding to which meetings the norms might apply and to which ones they wouldn't. I say they apply all the time to all meetings.   35F/UND

Alex: John, your expectations are that the norms apply to all meetings. Anyone have a different opinion? *[Pauses and looks at each person in succession. Each person indicates agreement.]* So much for one of the questions. Now back to Kim's original question. How do we want to use the norms?   36F/COM/RAT

Kim: I want to make a specific proposal. But before I do, I want to make it clear that, even though the norms will apply to all meetings, what I am going to propose will apply only to   37F/STR full team meetings. Meetings like this one, when everyone is expected to attend. I like Claire's idea. I propose that we try out the following procedure for the next month. First, before each meeting, we review the posted set of norms and make sure that they are still O.K. Second, anyone can ask that we use the norms at the end of any meeting to evaluate our performance. My assumption is that a person will ask that we evaluate ourselves against the norms because he or she thinks that we may not have adhered to all the norms.

Stella:	I like it.	**38F/COM** (Agreement)
John:	Trying it for a month sure won't kill us. I say let's do what Kim suggests.	**39F/COM** (Agreement)
Claire:	There's a lot of power in the idea of calling for a team evaluation at the end of any meeting. It sort of has the effect of keeping us on our toes.	**40F/UND**
Mat:	Just so we're clear that what Kim is proposing only applies to full team meetings.	**41F/UND**
Alex:	Anybody want to comment further on Kim's proposal? *[Pauses.]* Are we all agreed? Just so there is no misunder-	**42F/COM** (Consensus)

standing, why don't you repeat your proposal one more time, Kim?

[Lights fade.]

SCENE THREE

[Setting is the same as Scene One.]

Alex: Norms were the first thing that I suggested we take care of. For the rest of this meeting, we'll conform to our norms. *[Goes to flip chart and turns to page that lists the following items: Set norms; Review the Model for Superior Team Meetings; Job of designated facilitator; Set outcomes for meeting; How to reach our outcomes.]* Can we proceed to the second item, "Review the Model?"   **43F/STR (Outcomes)**

Mat: I think we could get rid of your job in a hurry. We all went to the same training. We know what your job is.   **44NF**

Alex: Mat seems to think that we don't need to clarify any further the job of the designated facilitator because we already know what it is. I don't know what the rest of you think, but I know I would like to be very clear about what you expect of me.   **45F/STR(Roles)**

Kim: Knowing that I may just be tapped to be facilitator next time, I agree with Alex. I would like for us to nail down exactly what I will be expected to do.

46F/COM (Agreement)

John: Claire said it up front. Facilitating our meetings is the job of everyone at a meeting. We are talking about team-managed facilitation. I think that we already have been doing it. There's been a lot of shared facilitating already going in this meeting, as far as I can see.

47F/UND

Kim: I agree, but how about putting up a few bullets on the flip chart just to make sure we are all in agreement?

48F/RAP

Alex: Before we pick up on Kim's suggestion, let me remind you that we are still deciding what we will do next. We completed the norms. Look at the list again. *[Points to the flip chart.]* The second item on the chart is to "review the model." We are just about to start on the third item, "job of designated facilitator." Do you want to pick up on Kim's suggestion and put up some bullets that describe what we expect our designated facilitators to do? Or do you want to review the model?"

49F/RAP(Keeping Conscious)

Don: I really think, Kim, that the model pretty much tells us what the designated facilitator's job is. We're all trying to have a successful meeting. The Model for Successful Team Meetings gives us a picture of what a successful meeting looks like. It tells us what we have to take care of. The facilitator's job is to help us to take care of what we need to take care of in order to have a successful meeting. **50F/UND**

Mat: We might just take care of both items together. Why not look at the model and talk about the facilitator's job at the same time? I don't think we have to worry all that much about the designated facilitator's job anyway. We are all facilitators. That's the whole point. We are all responsible for following the model. It's just that now, at the beginning, we are using a designated facilitator to help us get into the swing of things. **51F/RAP**

Claire: I can't figure out why you want to complicate everything, Mat. Why can't we just get on with the program? **52NF**

Mat: I'm not trying to complicate anything. I'm really trying to save time. I just think we are further along than **53F/UND**

maybe you do and that we can get through some of these preliminaries quickly.

Kim: I can live with Mat's idea. Let's look at the model and discuss what the designated facilitator or any of us should be doing to help us touch all the bases. **54F/COM**

Alex: So much for my list. Maybe the first rule for the designated facilitator is "never make a list." Oh well, I have very little pride of authorship anyway. Is everyone agreed that we will look at the model and just note as we go along what each element in the model means for facilitation? How about you, Claire? **55F/COM**

Claire: I'm prepared to go along with the team. I'm still not sure that we can manage to talk about facilitation and the model at the same time, but I'm willing to give it a try. **56F/COM**

Stella: We can try it and if we get bogged down, we can try something else. **57F/COM**

Mat: At the risk of rolling over anyone's objections, let's look at the model. I've brought along a copy for everyone. I think I can sketch it out, but the rest of you can keep me honest. **58F/RES/UND**

[Goes to the flip chart and draws the Model for Successful Team Meetings.]

[Lights fade.]

SCENE FOUR

[Setting is the same as before.]

Alex: I guess we have pretty much agreed **59F/UND** that the job of the designated facilitator and everyone else is to: one, help us take care of structuring ourselves—setting norms and that sort of thing; two, identify and use our resources—especially all of us at a meeting; three, follow logical steps or processes in everything we do—like what we've been doing so far at this meeting; four, communicate with one another in useful ways, such as being concrete, staying on the subject—that sort of thing; and five, keep us conscious of what we are doing at all times. For me, that last point is what makes it all hang together. I need one more question answered. How uninvolved am I suppose to be in what's going on? Do you want me to join in the discussion when I have an opinion or information or an idea?

Don: I think you should be involved as much as you can. You just have to keep one eye on the rest of us. 60F/UND

Claire: If we want someone who will not be involved and focus only on facilitating a meeting, then we can always get one from inside or outside the company. You shouldn't stop being a team member just because you may be the designated facilitator. 61F/UND

Stella: I think the designated facilitator is a team member with just one more job. Does that answer your question, Alex? 62F/UND

Alex: For the time being. If it doesn't work, we can change the rules. 63F/UND

Stella: I'd say you have been doing a pretty good job of keeping us conscious during this meeting. I can remember a couple of times already that we would have forgotten what we set out to do and started doing something else. 64F/UND

Kim: We didn't ever get around to listing the duties or functions of the designated facilitator. But now I don't think that we have to. We know what we have to do to have a successful team meeting. Whoever is facilitating, 65F/UND designated or not, has the job of helping us to make the model come to life.

Alex: Maybe we are ready to talk about what we want to produce at this meeting. I guess we already have produced several results. We have a set of norms. We have agreed on how we will use the norms for at least the next month. And we've agreed about facilitation and the job of all of us as facilitators. We have another thirty minutes before we call it quits. Are we ready to identify additional results for this meeting? **66F/UND**

John: I think we only have time to start listing what we want to achieve the next time we meet. I know I have a few items that I think we need to start looking at. One big one, of course, is how we are going to make the transition with all of our software into a "windows" environment. **67NF**

Mat: When are we going to meet anyway? Are we going to still have the Monday morning staff meetings? Are these team meetings in addition to all the other meetings that we have been having? **68NF**

Stella: Mat has a good point that we need to clarify. Dr. Alethos has made it clear that this company is headed in a big way toward a total team environment. I have been operating under the assumption that we need to have some special team meetings to push us along the road to improving ourselves as a team. We need special meetings to make this happen. That's what this meeting has been all about. That's what the training we had was all about. We need to have meetings to improve ourselves as a team. That means to me that we meet as a team anytime we need to do something together. **69F/UND**

Claire: It's clear that we are going to run out of time quickly now. I suggest that we select one task to work on for the rest of the time. I would like to see us work on what Mat and Stella have brought up. Let's decide what we mean by a team meeting, what we expect to do at these meetings, and when we plan to hold them. **70F/STR**

Alex: We probably can't take on much more at this meeting. Does anyone have an idea other than working on a single item for the rest of this meeting—that **71F/STR**

is, deciding about the purpose and frequency of our team meetings?

John: I think we have a couple of things that we need to be clear about when we start talking about teams.... 72NF

Kim: [Interrupting.] Hold on a minute John, let's decide if team meeting is the topic before we start discussing it. I think we should. How about the rest of you? 73F/STR(Keeping Conscious)

[Everyone acknowledges and agrees.]

Alex: We will need to leave time to complete our Team Evaluation Sheets and look at the results. So that gives us about twenty minutes to work on our questions about our team meetings. Let's see if we can identify what we want answered or the decisions we need to make. I think we might try going around the table and collecting each person's most important question and then go from there. Mat, you can start us off. [Alex goes to the flip chart and begins to jot down an abbreviated version of what each person says.] 74F/STR

Mat: I want to know if we are setting up a new meeting that we haven't had 75F/UND before—one that is supposed to serve a new purpose.

John: That's pretty much my question: are we going to start having some sort of special team meeting that is in addition to what we already do?   **76F/UND**

Don: I have the same question.   **77F/UND**

Kim: I want us to answer the first two questions that I've heard. First, are we having special team meetings? Two, what will be their purpose? But I also want to find out how often we intend to meet.   **78F/COM/UND**

Claire: If we can answer those three, it will take care of my questions.   **79F/COM**

Stella: I have nothing to add.   **80F/COM**

Alex: *[Turns to a clean sheet on the flip chart and writes as he talks.]* Kim already has summarized what the rest of you have said, I think. You want to make the following decisions: One, do we intend to start having special team meetings? I suppose the one we are now having would be called special. Second, what will be our purposes in meeting? Third, how often will we meet?   **81F/RAP**

Kim: Meeting together is one of the ways **82F/UND** that we can develop ourselves as a team. Also, it's one way that we can work on projects and goals to improve the whole team's performance. It's clear to me that the answer to the first question must be a "yes." Yes, we will have special team meetings. The answer to the second question is in the answer to the first. We need to meet to do something special, to improve ourselves as a team and every aspect of our work.

Mat: When we say that we are going to **83F/UND/COM** have a "team meeting," is there no doubt in everyone's mind that this is a special meeting? Is that the way the rest of you see it?

John: Anybody who thinks that teams and **84F/UND** teamwork are optional in this company has been badly misinformed. Stella is going to be evaluated on how well she builds us into a team. I can't imagine that meetings like this are not high on her priority list.

Stella: It is true that I am expected to build **85F/UND** CAT into a high performing team. But that's what I also expect of each of you. I'm sure that we will need to do a lot of things to make ourselves into such a team. I think that meeting regularly as a team is critical to improving our performance as a team.

Claire: I think we need a little reality check here. Is there anyone on this team who doesn't expect us to meet as a team on a regular basis? It looks to me as if we've already answered the first question. **86F/UND**

Mat: I take it that we are all agreed that we will have regular team meetings. Is that what we are going to call them: "team meetings?" **87F/COM/UND**

Kim: Suits me. Everyone O.K. with this? We will have meetings like the one we are in at the moment. And we will call them "team meetings" so that there is no doubt that these are not design reviews or routine staff meetings and the like. **88F/COM**

Alex: Does anyone have anything to add? All agreed? I think we've heard from everyone. How about the next question? What are the purposes of our meeting? **89F/COM/RAP**

John: The purposes are improvement— doing things together that we can't do without everyone being involved. **90F/UND**

Claire: I'd like to make it just a tad more concrete. I say we use these team meetings to improve our performance in at least the following areas: developing ourselves as a team (becoming more cooperative, responsive, and that sort of thing); identifying all our customers inside and outside the company and improving how satisfied they are with what we deliver; and improving all our work flows and processes (how we troubleshoot, respond to network problems, and that sort of thing). And I think we ought to work on improving the performance of our own suppliers. Anyhow, you get my drift. The purpose of our meetings should be to improve something. 91F/UND

Mat: Does that include planning, setting goals, solving technical problems? Is there any limit? 92F/UND

Stella: The answer for me is "yes" to all of the above and "no," I don't know how to limit what we might work on as a team at our team meetings. 93F/UND

Kim: I think we are ready to go to question three: how often do we meet? 94F/RAP

Alex: Everyone agree with Kim? How about Claire's description of our 95F/COM/UND purposes? *[Pauses and looks at each member.]*

Don: We've agreed to the following: We meet as a team. We call these meetings "team meetings." These meetings are different from all other meetings. These team meetings will be our time to work as a full team to develop ourselves as a team and to improve everything possible about our performance. It looks as if we are ready to answer the question about when we meet.   **96F/UND/RAP**

Mat: I think we ought to set a schedule for at least a couple of months and then decide again after that about our meetings. I am pretty green at this sort of thing and need to experiment and see what happens.   **97F/RAP**

John: It makes sense to put limits on what we try out. I suggest that we start meeting for two hours once a week. I think two months is a reasonable period to test the idea. Anyone want to do it differently?   **98F/STR/COM**

[Everyone agrees to John's suggestion to meet once a month for two hours.]

Alex: How about making it on a Friday from two to four in the afternoon?   **99F/UND/COM**

[Pauses.] Looks like everyone agrees. Then we'll pick it up again this Friday at two o'clock.

John: How about each of us bringing a list of problems or improvement opportunities to use at the next session? **100F/RES**

Don: Good idea.

Alex: We have just one last thing to do before we pack it in. *[Distributes the Team Evaluation Form as he continues to speak.]* Let's complete this and talk about it. **101/RAP/STR**

(Evaluation)

[Lights fade.]

SUMMARY OF CHAPTER'S KEY POINTS

This dramatization models some of the typical behaviors that we can expect from teams that understand and use team-managed facilitation based on the Model for Successful Team Meetings. In Chapter Four, we return to the Computer Assistance Team to illustrate further what team-managed facilitation looks like and the core competencies of facilitators. The key points that should be remembered from the dramatization are:

1. The Model for Successful Team Meetings is the primary tool for team-managed facilitation.

2. Any member of a team can and should facilitate the team's meetings.

3. Each team will define for itself the precise role of its designated facilitator. How involved or uninvolved a designated facilitator will be cannot be defined in the abstract.

4. Keeping the team conscious of what it is doing at all times is a large part of facilitation.

5. Communication during a meeting is most useful when it is: appropriate, factual, accurate, respectful, and team-centered.

6. Getting started is not easy for any group that wants to function as a team, but it is much easier when the team understands and uses the Model for Successful Team Meetings and team-managed facilitation.

Chapter 4

Core Competencies for Team-Managed Facilitation

This chapter presents in detail the sets of competencies that are required for successful facilitation and illustrates them with examples from the behavioral dramatization in Chapter 3.

INTERVENTION AS COMMUNICATION

Interventions by team members and designated facilitators during a team meeting can be thought of as communication behaviors. When we facilitate meetings, we say things and write things on flip charts or blackboards. What we say and write have the following purposes: first, to build meetings that conform to the Model for Successful Team Meetings; second, to help the team stay conscious of what it is doing; and, third, to add value to the communication of team members. The model is the plan, team members and designated facilitators are the builders, and the communication behaviors of everyone present during a meeting provide most of the material from which the meeting is constructed.

There are four sets of core competencies that people must master in order to become proficient in team-managed facilitation (see Figure 2-3). These are:

- Using the model;
- Keeping the team conscious;
- Modeling quality communication; and
- Listening to understand.

CORE COMPETENCY SET ONE: USING THE MODEL

Team-managed facilitation starts with a thorough grounding in the Model for Successful Team Meetings. The specific uses of the model for facilitation are:

1. Setting mental goals for the team so that facilitation is directed toward a set of intermediate and final goals; and

2. Using the model to guide interventions, i.e. communicating by design.

Setting Goals

The Model for Successful Team Meetings is used to set intermediate and final goals or outcomes for a meeting. Using team-managed facilitation means to be goal directed. Interventions should not be governed by whim and intuition. They should be based on a clear perception of what a team needs to take care of in order to achieve the successful results of task performance, team development, and improved meetings. To reach these goals, team members and designated facilitators will take action to help the team to reach whatever enabling goals are necessary (e.g., getting and using resources, designing clear structures, defining and using rational processes, and communicating).

People who use team-managed facilitation have an agenda. That agenda is to help the team to approximate as closely as possible the Model for Successful Team Meetings.

In the behavioral dramatization of team-managed facilitation in Chapter 3, there are numerous examples of the designated facilitator (Alex) and other team members providing input that is intended to help the team to use the model to conduct its meeting. The inputs of various team members illustrate their determination to fulfill the model's expectations regarding resources, structures, rational processes, and communication. The following examples from Scene One are interventions that are based on the model.

1F: The team leader, Stella, is consciously establishing the role of the designated facilitator. This input has the goal of providing *structure* to the meeting.

2F: Input to ensure that *resources* are available.

3F: Alex (the designated facilitator) has the goal of providing *structure* by establishing the expected outcomes of the meeting.

4F: Input establishes time and seating arrangement as *resources*.

6F: Alex's goal is to facilitate the team's communication by ensuring that all members have their say about the norms.

9F: Another input by Alex directed toward ensuring full *communication* about norms. At this point, even though the team has not yet established consensus as a norm for making decisions, Alex is operating on the assumption that this is the only way to agree on team norms.

14F: Alex is trying to help the team members to agree on a *rational process* by which to address other possible outcomes.

Using the Model To Guide Interventions, i.e., Communicating by Design

People who are trained in team-managed facilitation operate against a set of benchmarks. The benchmarks are the elements in the Model for Successful Team Meetings. The interventions that facilitators make are guided by the model, and the mental goals that they have set are based on the model.

Interventions by team members and the designated facilitator result from real-time assessments during the meeting of what the team is doing and how that compares to the model, i.e., what the team should be doing. Every team member or designated facilitator operates with a mental image of how the team should be performing.

As the team meeting takes place, members who know the meaning of team-managed facilitation make judgments. These judgments are based on a series of questions that depend on a knowledge of the Model for Successful Team Meetings and an intention to order personal communication during the meeting, based on the model.

The following are the types of questions that should be in the minds of team members and designated facilitators during a team meeting:

Concerning Resources:

- Has the team adequately identified the resources that it needs to do its work?
- Has the team obtained the right resources to do its work?
- Is the team fully using its resources, e.g., of time and people?

Concerning Structures:

- Has the team established clear outputs for the meeting?
- Has the team taken care of the basics such as norms, roles, general purposes of meetings, time and frequency of meetings, relationships to other meetings, and relationships to other team meetings and team-development activities within the organization?
- Is the team adequately identifying its developing needs to build new structures and modify old structures as it proceeds?
- Are team members fully conscious of the structures they have established and how they are using them?

Concerning Rational Processes:

- Is the team following a sequential and rational sequence for its meeting?
- As the team approaches each subtask or event during its meeting, has it determined exactly how it will proceed?
- Is the team sticking to the rational process that it has established to conduct its entire meeting or a specific task within the meeting?
- Is the team remaining conscious of how it is using its processes?

Concerning Communication:

- Are team members providing input that is appropriate, concrete, respectful, and team centered?
- Is each person fully involved in the topic being discussed and the decisions being made?

- Are team members fully conscious of how they are communicating—what they are doing that is useful and what they are doing that is dysfunctional?

Concerning Understanding:

- Has the topic, issue, or problem been well-defined so that all team members understand it?
- Has sufficient information been developed about the topic, issue, or problem?
- Are different opinions and options being developed and explored?

The sequential steps that the facilitator follows in making an intervention are: (1) mentally picture the model or conceptualize its key elements; (2) observe what actually exists or is occurring during the team meeting; (3) note the difference between "what actually is" and "what should be;" and (4) make an intervention.

The first set of core competencies required of people using team-managed facilitation is the ability to use the model to help the team to build the four key elements of the model (resources, structures, processes, and communication) into the meetings. The second set of core competencies for team-managed facilitation relate to keeping the team conscious.

CORE COMPETENCY SET TWO: KEEPING THE TEAM CONSCIOUS

The operational phrase here is "at all times." Team-managed facilitation is built on the premise that it is the team that is responsible for its own facilitation. For the team to act responsibly, it must be fully conscious of what it is doing at all times.

Anyone who has observed the performance of teams during their meetings knows how easy it is for teams "to go unconscious." It takes a great deal of personal discipline for any individual to remain fully aware of what he or she is doing in the process of interacting with just one other individual. Most of us do not know (during the moments of interaction) exactly what we are doing, much less what the impact of what we are doing is having on the other person. The process of "being unconscious" or "going unconscious" is much more pronounced and much more likely during meetings that involve several people.

Team meetings (like all human and natural systems) will move toward chaos and entropy unless they are infused with new information or energy. Facilitative interventions provide such information and energy.

In my analysis of just why teams so often "go random" and lose track of what they are doing or what they set out to do, I have discovered that the following reasons are the most pervasive:

1. **Complexity of a problem.** A team can get lost when it is trying to manage a number of variables at the same time. It can create a maze of diverging inputs and produce mountains of communication litter.

2. **Self-centeredness.** A team easily can "go unconscious" when its meetings are dominated by people who fail to develop or maintain their commitment to the *team's* tasks and success. Such people are concerned only to speak their own minds, give their own opinions, or obtain acceptance of their own proposals.

People make input and react to the input of others without weighing the value that such input has in relation to the team's tasks and goals.

3. **No model.** When teams meet without having agreed on the characteristics of a successful meeting, they will repeatedly lose consciousness of what they are doing and how well they are doing. With no standard by which to assess their performance, they have no way to develop and maintain team consciousness.

The primary behavioral characteristic that teams demonstrate when they lose consciousness is that the communication of members becomes more and more random. Inputs by team members have fewer and fewer of the characteristics associated with facilitative communication: that it is appropriate, concrete, respectful, and team centered.

Most people think about what they want to say, how they want to say it, and how they are saying it, rather than about *what* the team needs to have said and *when* it needs to have it said.

A major competency in team-managed facilitation is to keep the team conscious at all times of what it is doing. The consciousness of teams operates at two levels: (1) how aware any individual is at any moment of exactly what he or she is doing; and (2) how aware the collective body of the team is of what it is doing.

The following are two examples from the behavioral dramatization in Chapter 3 that illustrate communication to keep a team conscious.

25F: In this facilitative input, Alex reminds the team that it has branched off from the topic or issue that it was discussing onto another topic. The effect of

Alex's intervention is to help the team to make a conscious decision about the proposals made by Kim, Mat, and Claire about using the norms. Notice what could have happened if no one had made the team conscious at this point of what it was doing. It could have lost track of both Kim's and Claire's proposals and proceeded to discuss Mat's question about when the norms could be used. When teams lose consciousness, they inevitably waste time and, often, leave members with a sense of frustration over lack of efficiency and accomplishment.

66F: This comment by Alex summarizes for the team what it has just done, reminds the team of what it is now doing, and keeps the team aware of the amount of time that it has left in its meeting.

I have discussed two sets of core competencies for facilitation: (1) using the model; and (2) keeping the team conscious. The third set of core competencies required in team-managed facilitation is modeling quality communication, i.e., communication that has certain functional characteristics.

CORE COMPETENCY SET THREE: MODELING QUALITY COMMUNICATION

The key characteristics of facilitative communication also are functional because they support quality communication among members during a team meeting. The key qualities of facilitative communication are that it is:

- **Appropriate.** Being both timely and relevant to what the team is trying to achieve.

- **Concrete.** Being accurate, being specific, using data, and giving examples.
- **Respectful.** Listening to what others say and trying to use what they say.
- **Team-centered.** Focusing on what the team wants to accomplish rather than on what "I" want to accomplish. Serving the team's needs rather than personal needs.

Communication that does not have these characteristics will be nonfacilitative (i.e., will do no discernable good or actually will create blocks to the team's performance).

Appropriate

Communication that is appropriate is both *timely* and *relevant* to what the team is trying to achieve. In the behavioral dramatization in Chapter 3, all the inputs that are marked with "F" meet all the qualitative criteria of facilitative communication. The following examples have been selected to illustrate the quality of being appropriate.

8F: The team is still discussing norms. Kim's proposal is timely. She has not waited until the team has moved on to something else. Her comment is relevant to the topic of norms and contributes a new alternative.

12F: Stella's proposal has the same characteristics as Kim's (8F).

14F: Alex's comment is timely, because the team has just begun to lose its way—to become unconscious of the process it is following. The comment is relevant to the most important business at hand, which at this moment is not the task of developing and using norms but is the team's failure to follow a rational process.

Concrete

This criterion conveys the idea that team members are responsible for speaking as carefully as they can about what can be known. This does not mean that opinions are not useful. But even opinions can be wildly uninformed, self-serving, and too general to be applied. Concrete inputs also respond directly to the questions and issues at hand. Concreteness and obliqueness are not compatible. Examples of concrete input from the dramatization in Chapter 3 are:

23F: The questions that Mat raises are questions about facts related to how the norms will be used.

25F: This is a factual and accurate description of what has been going on and how the team has lost consciousness.

30F: This is a clear challenge to the team to understand the issue that it is discussing. The discussion is forced to become more concrete when the team is asked to look at the facts related to its meetings and its use of the norms.

37F: Kim specifies clearly how her proposal will apply and what the proposal is.

69F: Stella clearly relates what is expected by Dr. Alethos and why there is a need for special team meetings.

Respectful

Respectful communication by team members is communication that stimulates the free and open development of information and does nothing to inhibit this development. This does not mean that disagreement is to be avoided. Disagreement is absolutely necessary in order for teams to develop all the information they need and to make their best decisions. Energetic disagreement is typical among superior teams (Kinlaw, 1991).

There are a few common ways of communicating non-respect that team members should always avoid. These behaviors are described below.

1. **Generalizing.** This is communication that goes beyond the facts and is not accurate. It includes statements such as the following:

   - "None of you seems to want to understand what I am saying."
   - "You always seem to look for reasons that we should not do something rather than looking for reasons that we should."

2. **Ridiculing.** These are behaviors that exaggerate a person's apparent shortcomings. For example:

   - "Congratulations, Nathan, I can only conclude from that last statement of yours that you intended to find the most creative way possible to make the whole team look like fools to the Vice President."
   - "You are about as well-organized as a busted beehive."

3. **Being judgmental.** This is communication that is critical of a person's intentions or reduces the value of others' contributions to zero or near zero. Judgmental statements usually carry an element of blame.

   - "If you didn't think that you could support the team's decision, why did you act as if you were going along with it?"
   - "Maybe the reason that you believe that your ideas are not being taken seriously by the rest of us is that

you don't present them so that we can understand them."

Respectful communication tends to minimize reactions of *resistance* or *resentment*, both of which block the free exchange of opinion and information.

All the facilitative inputs (marked "F") in the dramatization in Chapter 3 are respectful. The nonfacilitative inputs (marked "NF") are not.

The first three qualities of facilitative communication are that it is appropriate, concrete, and respectful. The fourth characteristic is that it is team-centered.

Team-Centered

Facilitative communication centers on what the team needs to do, not on what individual members need to say. Team-centered communication focuses on the team's tasks, not on the quirks and flaws of its members. Team-centered communication is about getting the team's job done. Team-centered communication requires that team members stay fully conscious of what the team is doing. The following are examples from the dramatization in Chapter 3 of team-centered (facilitative) communication:

25F: Comments such as this one, which keep the team conscious, are clearly team-centered. Other examples are **49F** and **73F**.

2F: Inputs that urge the team to focus on desired outcomes are team-centered. Another example is **43F**.

6F: Inputs such as this one, which test for consensus or lead the team toward consensus, are team-centered. Other examples are **9F, 12F, 13F,** and **16F**.

Examples of Nonfacilitation

The behavioral dramatization in Chapter 3 contains a few inputs that are nonfacilitative. These nonfacilitative inputs reflect, in varying degrees, what the team member wants to say, rather than a clear understanding of what would help the team. For example:

5NF: Mat's input is focused on his own need to express his opinion. It is not concrete, probably not respectful, and certainly not team centered. It does little to help the team to understand and perform its task. It is, however, disagreement. To the extent that it helps the team to encourage, accept, and use disagreement, it may have some value.

10NF: This input probably is not hurtful to the team's efficiency but it does nothing directly to assist the team. It communicates more about Claire's impatience than it does anything else. Again, it is not the disagreement that is unhelpful; it is the poor quality of the comment that is the problem.

18NF: This comment is a disguised disagreement rather than a statement of agreement. It is not concrete or team centered.

21NF: This comment borders on sarcasm. It does not help much.

44NF: Here is another comment that reflects personal impatience. It is not team centered.

52NF: This input is an attack at Mat. It does not meet any of the criteria for facilitative communication. It is not respectful.

67NF: John's comment demonstrates that he has lost sight of the team's agenda and process and is now most concerned about his need to have the company's transition to a "windows environment" discussed. John starts out to set up a rational process but then begins to list issues before the team has agreed to the process. He tends to focus on a single issue before all issues have been identified. This is not appropriate.

68NF: Mat does not respond to John or to the structure that Alex is trying to build. His input is an undisciplined response to his own concerns. This shifts the team from listing what it wants to achieve at its next meeting to the topic of when the team will meet. It is not appropriate. A more useful input would have been to acknowledge that the team was about to discuss its next agenda and then to indicate that time should be allowed to discuss the schedule for the next meeting. Stella is able, however, to use Mat's input to help the team develop a better understanding of the need for team meetings.

72NF: This input (if left alone) could shift the team into a discussion of another topic rather than staying conscious of the topic of when and why to meet. It is not appropriate.

NORMS AND COMMUNICATION

One of the proven ways to support the regular use of facilitative communication during team meetings is to specify in the team's meeting norms, as carefully as possible, exactly what kind of communication is expected. Figure 4-1 is an example of norms for team communication.

Just as the Model for Successful Team Meetings helps team members to anticipate what they must do to facilitate a meeting and provides a benchmark for evaluating the

- Listen and, before you speak, make sure that you have understood what the persons who spoke before you meant.

- Pay careful attention to how much you talk and ensure that there is a balanced dialog among members.

- Always take the input of other members seriously. Don't discount or ridicule it.

- Don't let the input of the person who speaks before you get lost or not be responded to by the team.

- Take time periodically to summarize what has been said during a meeting.

- Be as conscious of helping others to make a contribution as you are of the things you want to say.

- Be candid. Confront others when you disagree.

- Do not ever act as though you agree when you do not.

- Stay concrete and factual. Avoid generalizing.

- Keep your remarks focused on the task or topic at hand.

Figure 4-1: Team-Meeting Communication Norms

team's performance during a meeting, so a set of communication norms makes team members conscious of how they are expected to communicate during a meeting and provides a tool for evaluating their communication during and after a meeting.

The communication skills required for facilitation help to keep inputs appropriate, concrete, respectful, and team-centered. There is one skill that underlies most of the other skills. This skill ensures that the facilitator's interventions are appropriate (i.e., timely and relevant). It ensures that the facilitator keeps the team conscious and also helps team members to maintain high quality in their communications with one another. This skill, not surprisingly, is listening to understand.

CORE COMPETENCY SET FOUR: LISTENING TO UNDERSTAND

Listening as a skill in team-managed facilitation means listening to understand. It means to listen to determine such things as:

- How well is the team developing the primary elements required for a successful meeting: resources, structures, rational processes, communication, and understanding?
- How conscious is the team of what it is doing?
- What is the quality of the communication among team members?

Listening to understand requires that facilitators develop the discipline to:

- Listen *only* to what another person is communicating, rather than to what they want to find in that communication;

- Treat the communication of others as information without trying to evaluate that communication as right or wrong and without trying to force it into the framework of their own concerns and needs.

Most people probably have had the following experiences during a team meeting:

- Other members have responded to a question that I asked by answering another question that I did not ask. I ended up getting information that I didn't need and not getting information that I did need. The problem here is that people were finding what they wanted to find in my communication, rather than just listening to what I was saying.
- Other members have asked me for my opinion about an issue, but when I gave it, they let me know that they didn't like it or that it was wrong or of no value. The problem here is that people were so busy *evaluating* what they thought I was saying that they couldn't *hear* what I was saying.

The goal of listening is to understand. Understanding is related to the amount of information that the team develops around an issue or problem. There are a few well-known skills that force us to listen and, at the same time, stimulate the development of information by other team members. These skills are acknowledging, reflecting, and summarizing (Kinlaw, 1989).

Acknowledging

Acknowledging includes all the "grunts" and "groans" that communicate to another person that I am involved in what he or she is saying. Examples are:

Team-Managed Facilitation

- "Yes, I can understand that."
- "Right."
- "Uh huh."
- "I can see that."
- "I've heard of that."

Acknowledging behavior stimulates others to continue to provide information. Such behavior also helps to force facilitators to listen and not to interrupt.

Examples of acknowledging behavior from the dramatization are:

32F: "Stella sure knows how she feels about the norms."

77F: "I have the same question."

80F: "I have nothing to add."

Reflecting

The skill of reflecting describes responses that briefly restate what another team member has said or what the other team member is feeling. Reflecting does not mean *interpreting* what the other person has said. Also, reflecting does not mean *parroting* what the other person has said. Reflecting means *to restate in one's own words* what the other person has said in order to convey understanding of what the other person has said. Such responses communicate understanding and encourage the development of information. Some examples of statements and reflecting responses are found below.

Input: "I don't really understand what good it is to spend all this time on norms. We'll never take the time to use them anyway."

Reflecting: "Seems to you this could be a waste of time or at least you're not sure that we will benefit very much."

Input: "With all these changes hitting us at once, we're headed for mass confusion. We're being told to empower everybody, manage differently, work with our customers differently, and a ton of other things."

Reflecting: "From where you sit, it feels like there are no answers to anything right now, just questions."

Reflecting is a skill that most of us do not grow up using "naturally." But it is a very useful skill in team-managed facilitation, for the following reasons.

- To reflect, you must listen. Reflecting forces listening and builds strong listening skills. You cannot restate or convey understanding of another's feelings unless you have first heard accurately what the other person has said and observed accurately what the other person is feeling.
- The beauty of reflecting responses is that they develop information even when they are not quite accurate or on target. When a reflecting response is off target, the other team member will respond with a "no" and then clarify what she or he has said.

Examples of reflecting behavior from the dramatization in Chapter 3 are:

36F: "John, your expectations are that the norms apply to all meetings."

45F: "Mat seems to think that we don't need to clarify any further the job of the designated facilitator because we already know what it is."

Team-Managed Facilitation

Acknowledging and reflecting are particularly useful listening skills. A third listening skill is summarizing.

Summarizing

A good facilitating technique is to stop the development of information periodically and summarize the information a team has developed up to that point. This intervention helps the team to stay conscious of what it is doing. It also helps team members to keep in mind the key facts, and it ensures that the team's conversation progresses with mutual understanding.

Examples of summarizing are:

- "The outcomes that we have identified so far for this meeting are: to identify our internal and external customers; to select the customers that are most important to us at the moment; and to develop a set of satisfiers for each customer."

- "We have now agreed that we will use our team-meeting norms in the following ways: review them before each meeting, refer to them during a meeting if we start to violate any of them, and use them at the end of at least every second meeting to evaluate our overall performance."

Examples of summarizing from the dramatization are:

59F: "I guess we have pretty much agreed that the job of the designated facilitator and everyone else is to: One, help us take care of structuring ourselves—setting norms and that sort of thing; two, identify and use our resources—especially all of us at a meeting; three, follow logical steps or processes in everything we do—like what we've been doing so far at this meeting; four, communicate with one another in useful ways, such as being concrete, staying on the subject—that sort of thing; and five, keep us conscious of what we are doing at all times."

96F: "We've agreed to the following: We meet as a team. We call these meetings 'team meetings.' These meetings are different from all other meetings. These team meetings will be our time to work as a full team to develop ourselves as a team and to improve everything possible about our performance."

SUMMARY OF CHAPTER'S KEY POINTS

This chapter has described the core competencies that facilitators must develop to be fully successful. The key points related to competencies are summarized below.

1. There are four sets of core competencies that people must master to use team-managed facilitation. These sets of core competencies are:

    - Using the model;
    - Keeping the team conscious;
    - Modeling quality communication; and
    - Listening to understand.

2. **Core Competency Set One: Using The Model.** Team-managed facilitation starts with a thorough grounding in the Model for Successful Team Meetings. Everything about team-managed facilitation depends on the model and is derived from it. The

specific uses of the model for facilitation are: (1) setting mental goals for the team so that facilitation is directed toward a set of intermediate and final goals; and (2) using the model to guide interventions.

3. **Core Competency Set Two: Keeping The Team Conscious**. Team-managed facilitation is based on the premise that it is the team that is responsible for its own facilitation. For the team to act responsibly, it must be fully conscious of what it is doing at all times.

4. **Core Competency Set Three: Modeling Quality Communication.** Facilitative communication is appropriate, concrete, respectful, and team centered.

5. **Core Competency Set Four: Listening To Understand.** Listening to understand means to listen to determine such things as:

   ■ How well is the team developing the primary elements required for a successful meeting, i.e., resources, structures, rational processes, communication, and understanding?

   ■ How conscious is the team of what it is doing?

   ■ What is the quality of the communication among team members?

   Listening to understand requires that facilitators develop the discipline to:

   ■ Listen only to what another person is communicating, rather than to what they want to find in that communication;

   ■ Treat the communication of others as information, without trying to evaluate that communication as right or wrong or to force it into the framework of their own concerns and needs.

In addition, there are a few well-known skills that force us to listen and (at the same time) stimulate the development of information by other team members. These skills are acknowledging, reflecting, and summarizing.

Chapter 5

Facilitation and the Roles of Leaders and Managers

The foregoing chapters of this book describe team-managed facilitation. This chapter covers the relationship of facilitation to the emerging roles and responsibilities of leaders and managers.

NEW ROLES FOR NEW LEADERS

Throughout this book, "facilitation" has meant the facilitation of team meetings. The concept has not been applied to the many other tasks that teams and team members must perform in order to carry out their missions and reach their goals. However, the characteristics and competencies associated with team-managed facilitation do have a wider application.

Team-managed facilitation employs competencies that are the same (or very similar) to the competencies that now are required of every organizational manager and leader. Therefore, facilitation (in the way in which it is described in this book) is one of the roles that any person who exercises a leadership role must learn to perform comfortably and competently.

It is now obvious that the traditional model of managing performance by control no longer is a very useful one. Sustained superior performance of organizations can be achieved only through the personal commitment of people to total quality.

The control model does not work for some very obvious reasons:

1. Most jobs are now so complex and require such a high level of technical competency that the people who perform the work know a great deal more about their jobs than their bosses know about these jobs. How can anyone presume to control the performance of others in such circumstances?

2. Successful performance in jobs more and more requires response to the unknown and the unexpected. The very complexity of work and the variability of work requirements make it less and less likely that managers and supervisors can know with confidence what the people who report to them should be doing. The whole notion of control is built on predictability. How can managers control the work of others when they often cannot know with confidence what these others should be doing?

3. People control more and more of their discretionary time or effort. Most people report that they could give at least fifteen percent less effort or time or fifteen percent more effort or time to their jobs and no one would know the difference (Kinlaw, 1989). How can the work of people be controlled when they often control so much discretionary time and effort?

4. People always have been known to work harder toward those goals and support more fully those decisions that they have helped to create. Participation (and now empowerment) is a proven strategy for gaining commitment and superior performance. Control never has been shown to be a strategy for producing sustained superior performance. Given the reality that only sustained superior performance can secure competitive position, we must look elsewhere for the management and leadership strategy that we require.

If leading and managing by control does not work, what strategy does work? The answer is a strategy to gain commitment! What achieves sustained superior performance, continuous improvement, total quality, competitive position, and market share is the commitment of people to do more than is asked, to respond before they are directed, and to improve every aspect of their work on their own initiative.

People always are the critical resource and the sufficient cause for improving an organization's performance. Technology, machines, and systems are only the tools. Improvement strategies always must focus on people.

We already have, for example, sufficient technology to reduce by at least fifty percent our energy consumption in all forms. What we do not have is the commitment of people to do it. We now have the technology to improve the performance of every single work process and the tools to measure such improvements (Kinlaw, 1992). What is still needed is the commitment of people to improve and measure their performance.

There are at least three management and leadership roles that clearly support the development of commitment. The first one, *coaching*, is discussed at length in *Coaching for Commitment: Managerial Strategies for Obtaining Superior Performance* (Kinlaw, 1989). The second role, *team developer*, is described in *Developing Superior Work Teams: Building Quality and the Competitive Edge* (Kinlaw, 1991). The third role is *facilitator*.

Leaders and managers today must be coaches—developers of people—through tutoring, mentoring, counseling, and challenging. They must also be developers of teams, through initiating actions to develop teams and modeling teamwork to others. But they must be more. Managers and leaders must see their most fundamental purpose as that of *making things easy* for all their co-workers. They must be *facilitators*.

The emerging roles of leaders and managers are driven by shifts in their required functions. The need for leaders and managers who are coaches, developers of teams, and facilitators of people's performance will become more and more pronounced as the function of leadership continues to shift:

- Away from a focus on "putting out fires" and "fixing what's broken" to focusing on systemic change and finding new ways to do business;
- Away from controlling people to helping them find higher and higher levels of personal and team influence;
- Away from communicating ideas to people to stimulating them to develop their own ideas;
- Away from focusing on individuals as primary work units to focusing on teams as primary work units;

- Away from concentrating on functional responsibilities to concentrating on process and system responsibilities;
- Away from encouraging internal competition to encouraging internal cooperation; and
- Away from directing people what to improve to helping them to search for and implement their own improvements.

When these shifts in the functions of managers and leaders are related to facilitation (as it has been described in this book), it becomes apparent that facilitation represents a set of competencies that are very congruent with these shifts in functions. One way in which leaders can equip themselves for their emerging roles is by understanding team-managed facilitation and becoming fully capable in the core competencies associated with team-managed facilitation.

The leader of the future will be skilled in facilitating every conversation to ensure that full use is made of the mental resources represented by all others involved. If we take the position that every meeting that a manager or leader has with one or more other persons is a potential team meeting (regardless of the degree of formality involved), the sets of core competencies of team-managed facilitation are applicable (in varying degrees) to any and all meetings. Leaders and managers must be able to:

- Use the Model for Successful Team Meetings;
- Keep the team conscious;
- Model quality communication; and
- Listen to understand.

Translated into specific behaviors during a conversation with one or more persons, leaders will consciously try to facilitate each interaction they have by:

- Helping to identify and use the resources required;
- Helping to give structure to the conversation so that everyone knows what the conversation should accomplish, what decisions must be made, and so on;
- Helping to keep the conversation moving in a logical, sequential way;
- Modeling good communication behavior; and
- Helping everyone involved in the conversation to develop a full understanding of all topics discussed.

They also will help all the people who are involved in a conversation to stay conscious of what they are doing by:

- Commenting when the conversation seems to become confused and sidetracked;
- Suggesting that important but unrelated topics and information introduced into the conversation be tagged for later discussions;
- Helping people to remain aware of their time limits; and
- Helping to keep input from being ignored and "falling through the cracks."

Leaders-as-facilitators will be models of useful conversation. They will strive to help people to keep their inputs appropriate, concrete, respectful, and focused on what the people in the conversation are trying to accomplish together.

Finally, leaders who will function most comfortably in the emerging environment of involvement, mutual influence, and teamwork will become masters at listening to understand. They will become disciplined in listening without judging and in the use of skills that develop information, such as reflecting and summarizing.

I am not proposing that the description of facilitation and the skills for team-managed facilitation provide a complete model of the kind of leadership that is becoming more and more required in today's organizations. I am suggesting that a good bit of what I have said about facilitation describes an understanding and skills that are peculiarly fitted to the emerging roles of organizational leadership.

CONCLUSION

We can expect that what we have seen in team formation and development in organizations to date is little more than a prelude to things to come. Organizations have only just begun to discover the energy and creative power that can be generated in the interactive communication networks that are characteristic of teams. In the future that is now unfolding, organizations will not be characterized just by *having* teams. They will be characterized by *being* teams.

The more that organizations become teams, the more they will be able to:

- Create, integrate, and use new ideas, knowledge, and wisdom;
- Develop and use the competencies of people;

- Make the most efficient uses of time, materials, equipment, and other resources;
- Increase each person's commitment to and ownership of the total performance of the organization; and
- Manage uncertainty and change.

Team-managed facilitation is a major organizational resource for stimulating and supporting team formation and for developing the self-sufficiency of teams. The emphasis is on *facilitation,* not on facilitators. The reason for this emphasis is to underscore the belief that facilitation represents a set of competencies that every member of an organization can learn.

I propose that we begin to understand facilitation in a new way, as a team-managed responsibility and activity. Organizations that translate this understanding into action and equip people with the skills for team-managed facilitation can expect to reap the benefits of team development, highly improved team meetings, and rapid strengthening of teams as self-sufficient units of performance. What is more, training people in team-managed facilitation is, at the same time, training them for a leadership role that we can expect to become more and more dominant—along with that of coach and developer of teams.

Appendix ⟩

Outline for Team-Managed-Facilitation Training

This book is the primary resource for designing and conducting team-managed-facilitation training. However, the training outline presented in this section represents but one of the many ways in which the content of the book can be used to design team-managed-facilitation training. The purpose of this appendix is not to provide a detailed description of a training program or a leader's guide but to provide an outline that is sufficiently complete to give guidance in designing such programs.

CORE MODULES

A typical program in team-managed facilitation will last a minimum of two days (or the equivalent) and include the following modules:

- Payoffs, Content, and Objectives;
- The Meaning of Team-Managed Facilitation;
- The Model for Successful Team Meetings;
- Review of a Behavioral Dramatization;
- Core Competencies; and
- Practice and Feedback.

Each of these training elements is discussed briefly in the following sections.

A TEAM-CENTERED DESIGN FOR TEAM-MANAGED-FACILITATION TRAINING

Team-managed facilitation can be taught best to teams. A training program will be most efficient and effective if people attend the training in the teams in which they presently are working or in which they will be working after the training.

Team-managed-facilitation training is based on the premise that teams should be responsible for their own facilitation and the success of their meetings. It is the whole team that is responsible and it is the team as a whole that should be trained. It is, of course, not always possible to have all members of a team present at the same time for the same training. But such an arrangement should be the goal.

Delivering training to individuals is always less desirable than delivering training to teams made up of the people who must work together to apply what is learned during the training. This is particularly true when the content of the training is directly concerned with the development and performance of teams. To design a training program in the skills of team development and performance and offer it to individuals who do not actually work together as a team is very inefficient. Such an arrangement misses a significant opportunity to use the training as a strategy for developing teams and for creating immediate results.

In those cases in which individuals are acquiring knowledge and skills that may apply directly to their job tasks, without reference to other people or involvement with them, training people as isolates is appropriate. However, all learning related to team formation, development, and performance must be applied by teams and, therefore, should take place in teams.

By training teams, we equip them to apply their learnings as teams. More importantly, by targeting the training for people who work together, we give them the opportunity to apply their learning to themselves and their real world. We eliminate the need to show participants how to translate their learnings to the work environment. They have brought their work environment with them into the learning environment.

The following outline of a team-managed-facilitation training program generally requires two days to deliver. The amount of time actually required depends on the number of participants and how much practice each participant will have in functioning as a designated facilitator. The activities described as part of the outline assume that each participant has access to the material included in this book.

TRAINING OUTLINE

Module 1: Payoffs, Content, and Objectives

Payoffs. Team-managed-facilitation training has special organizational and individual payoffs that should be acknowledged at the beginning of the training. The major organizational payoffs are:

1. Improvement of the competency base for team formation and development throughout the organization;

2. Skill training that has broad application for leaders and other key personnel;

3. Further strengthening of the capacity of teams to manage their own development and performance; and

4. Improvement of the efficiency and effectiveness of all team meetings throughout the organization.

Payoffs for individuals and teams participating in the training are:

1. New competencies for making personal contributions to their teams' performance (as well as to other teams);

2. Tools to use for their ongoing development as facilitators; and

3. Further development of their leadership skills.

Content. The content of the program consists of the following modules:

- Learning the meaning and special characteristics of team-managed facilitation;
- Understanding and using the Model for Successful Team Meetings, which describes the key elements that must be managed in team meetings;
- Learning to discriminate between facilitative and nonfacilitative behavior by using a behavioral dramatization; and

■ Practicing the core facilitative skills.

Objectives. There are three primary training objectives. Participants should learn:

1. The special characteristics that distinguish team-managed facilitation from traditional forms of facilitation;

2. How to use the Model for Successful Team Meetings to facilitate meetings; and

3. The core skills of facilitation and a satisfactory level of competence in using them.

Module 2: The Meaning of Team-Managed Facilitation

This module contains a single activity: a presentation and discussion of the special characteristics of team-managed facilitation. This emphasizes that it is empirical, structured, explicit, thoroughly rational, and, most of all, *a responsibility of every team member.*

Module 3: The Model for Successful Team Meetings

This module has the sequence of activities described below.

Exercise. Request participants to think about small group meetings in which they recently have participated. Ask each person to jot down the events or factors that hindered or blocked the group's performance or success, i.e., what got in the way?

Next, in teams, have participants discuss their experiences and develop a list of blocks. Tell each team to reduce its list to the top five blocks and to write these on flip-chart paper, to be used later for discussion in the general session. Save these lists for use after a presentation of the Model for Successful Team Meetings.

Present the Model for Successful Team Meetings. Make a visual display of the model and discuss each of the elements. After presentation of the whole model, review each of the elements (resources, structures, rational processes, etc.) and have the participants classify the blocks that they have identified in the previous exercise.

Exercise. Have the participants work in teams to discuss the Model for Successful Team Meetings. Ask them to develop any questions that may result from their team discussions for further discussion at the general session.

How To Use the Model in Facilitation. The main objectives of this presentation and discussion are to provide the following:

1. A conceptual framework of facilitation to help teams to anticipate what they must do (i.e., the variables that they must manage) in order to have successful meetings;

2. A conceptual basis for identifying the competencies needed for the role of facilitator and for integrating these competencies into a unified and coherent body of knowledge;

3. A tool that can be used to evaluate the performance of teams at their meetings and to evaluate how well the designated facilitator of the meeting has done; and

4. A framework within which decisions can be made about what interventions should be used during a meeting and when they should be used.

Module 4: Review of Behavioral Dramatization

Chapter 3 contains a behavioral dramatization that models communication that is facilitative. In order to highlight the facilitative behaviors, a few nonfacilitative behaviors are included in the dramatization.

Exercise. Use Scene One. Ask the participants to work in teams to review the inputs in Scene One and the notes. The task is for them to ensure that they recognize that the notes accurately describe the behaviors. This exercise helps participants begin to recognize what facilitative and nonfacilitative behaviors look like. After the teams have discussed Scene One, ask them to bring any questions that they might have to the general session.

Module 5: Core Competencies

Present a brief overview of the sets of core competencies:

- Using the model;
- Keeping the team conscious;
- Communicating by design; and
- Listening to understand.

Using The Model. Discuss this competency set. Give examples from Scene Two from the dramatization.

Exercise. Use Scene Three from the dramatization. Have the participants work in teams. Cover the notes. The participants' task is to identify positive examples of behaviors that illustrate using the model to set mental goals and to structure interventions.

Keeping the Team Conscious. Discuss this competency set. Give examples from Scene Three from the dramatization.

Exercise. Use Scene Four from the dramatization. Have participants work in teams. Cover the notes. The participants' task is to identify positive examples of behaviors that illustrate keeping the team conscious.

Communication by Design. Discuss this competency set. Give examples from Scene Three from the dramatization.

Exercise. Use Scene Four from the dramatization. Have participants work in teams. Cover the notes. The participants' task is to identify positive examples of behaviors that illustrate using the model.

Listening To Understand. Discuss this competency set. Emphasize that facilitators must be good listeners if they are to know:

- How well the team is building the primary elements required for a successful meeting, i.e., resources, structures, rational processes, communication, and understanding;
- How conscious the team is of what it is doing; and
- What the quality of the communication among team members is.

Listening to understand requires the discipline to:

- Listen *only* to what another person is communicating rather than to what the listener wants to find in the communication; and
- Treat the communication of others as information without trying to evaluate that communication as right or wrong or to force it into the framework of the listener's concerns and needs.

Exercise. Discuss and give examples of the listening skills of acknowledging, reflecting, and summarizing. Have each team designate one member as an observer. Give the team the task of developing a list of what should be the company's top five strategic goals for the next five years. Task each member to try to use the listening skills as often as possible during the discussion. Tell the observer to record for each member how many times the member used one of the listening skills. Conclude the exercise by having the observer report his or her observations to the team. Repeat the exercise. Change observers. Assign teams the task of developing a list of the top seven criteria that should be used in selecting supervisors for promotion to the next level of management in the company.

Review the Sets of Core Competencies. List again each of the four competency sets and ensure that participants understand the functions of the four sets in facilitation.

Module 6: Practice and Feedback

Participants now have been exposed to the concepts and skills of team-managed facilitation. They have the Model for Successful Team Meetings to guide them. They have identified competencies and practiced listening to understand. The remainder of the program is devoted to practice and feedback. This module can be enriched by introducing various tools, such as the nominal group technique, cause-and-effect diagrams, flow charting, etc. Each iteration of practice exercises for designated facilitators can include the use of one such tool.

Have each team identify at least three topics or problems that it will use for practicing facilitation and successful team meetings. Suggested topics may include:

- Opportunities to improve customer satisfaction;
- Opportunities to improve work processes;
- Opportunities to improve supplier performance;
- Opportunities to improve team development; and
- Blocks to our best performance that we can remove.

Each participant should have at least two opportunities to serve as a designated facilitator.

Exercise. Repeat this exercise a sufficient number of times to give each participant at least two opportunities to serve as designated facilitator. The steps for the exercise are:

1. Each team determines the sequence in which each team member will serve as designated facilitator. From this point on, the designated facilitator begins to facilitate.
2. The team selects a topic.
3. The team selects one outcome that it wants to achieve through discussion of the topic.
4. The team conducts the discussion and tries to achieve the outcome within the time assigned.

5. At end of the time allowed for the discussion, the team evaluates itself by using the Team-Managed-Facilitation Evaluation Form (Figure 2-4). Next, the team gives feedback to the designated facilitator by using the Designated-Facilitator Evaluation Form (Figure 2-5).

Repeat the exercise. Each team may decide to continue the topic and process from the first iteration of the exercise or may select a new topic. This is the first task that the new designated facilitator will help the team to complete.

References and Resources

Bradford, L.P. (Ed.). (1978). *Group development.* San Diego, CA: Pfeiffer & Company.

Bradford, L.P. (1976). *Making meetings work: A guide for leaders and group members.* San Diego, CA: Pfeiffer & Company.

Bonner, H. (1959). *Group dynamics.* New York: Ronald Press.

Dewar, D.L. (1980). *Quality circle member manual.* Red Bluff, CA: Quality Circle Institute.

Glaser, R., & Glaser, G. (1985). *Group facilitators intervention guidebook* (2nd ed.). Bryn Mawr, PA: Organization Design and Development.

Kinlaw, D.C. (1989). *Coaching for commitment: Managerial strategies for obtaining superior performance.* San Diego, CA: Pfeiffer & Company.

Kinlaw, D.C. (1991). *Developing superior work teams: Building quality and the competitive edge.* New York: Lexington Books.

Kinlaw, D.C. (1992). *Continuous improvement and measurement for total quality: A team-based approach.* San Diego, CA: Pfeiffer & Company.

Mosvick, R.K., & Nelson, R.B. (1986). *We've got to start meeting like this: A guide to successful business meeting management.* Glenview, IL: Scott, Foresman.

Orsburn, J.D., et al. (1990). *Self-directed work teams: The new American challenge.* Homewood, IL: Business One Irwin.

Van Grundy, A.B. (1981). *Techniques of structured problem solving.* New York: Van Nostrand Reinhold.

Index

Intervention
definition, 17
Interventions, 12-13, 32-34, 102-
104, 106
a framework for, 64, 66

J

Johari Window, 10

K

Keeping conscious, 47-48, 72, 81,
86, 93, 100, 106-109
Kinlaw, 3, 5, 18, 22, 25, 28, 37, 56,
63, 118, 126, 128

L

Leader of the future, 129
Leaders
new roles, 107-112
Leaders and managers
roles of, 125-132
Leaders-as-facilitators, 130
Leadership, 57
Leading and managing by control,
127
Level of development, 28-29, 34
Level of difficulty, 34
Listening to understand, 47-48, 67,
72, 102, 117-123, 129, 139-141

M

Management teams, 27
Meetings, 24-25, 39
facilitation of, vi
Member facilitators, 9, 63, 72
Model for successful team meetings,
8-9, 13, 15, 17, 30, 31, 33, 35, 38-
39, 43-44, 46, 55, 58, 67-70, 72,
99-100, 103-104, 115
Mosvick & Nelson, 39, 42

N

NASA, 26
Network teams, 27
Nonfacilitation, 114-115
Norms, 50, 76, 79, 115-116

O

Orsburn, 25
Outcomes, 76, 85

P

Pareto diagram, 52
Performance, 24-25, 39, 44, 51, 55
managing by control, 126
Positive team feelings, 57
Potential, 44, 49, 55
Problem-solving process, 52
Processes, 51
Project teams, 27

Q

Quality communication, 109

R

Rational processes, 9, 41, 44, 52-53,
55-56, 68, 72-73, 105
Reflecting, 119-120
Resources, 41, 44, 49, 51, 55, 68,
72-73, 104
Respectful facilitative communica-
tion, 111-113
Results, 44, 55
Ridiculing, 112
Role of meetings in team develop-
ment and performance, 24-25
Roles, 1, 50, 85
Rotating the role to develop compe-
tence, 31

S

Self-evaluation, 31
Setting goals, 102
Special-improvement teams, 27
Structure, 41
Structures, 44, 46, 50-51, 53, 55, 68,
72, 105
Summarizing, 121-122

T

Task achievement, 55
Task performance, 55-56, 102